90

THE 90s—
A LOOK BACK

COMPILED BY

TONY HENDRA
AND
PETER ELBLING

DESIGNED BY

KOPPEL & SCHER

AVON BOOKS ◆ NEW YORK

THE 90'S: A LOOK BACK
is an original publication
of Avon Books.
This work has never before
appeared in book form.

AVON BOOKS
A division of
The Hearst Corporation
105 Madison Avenue
New York, New York
10016

Copyright © 1989
by Tony Hendra and
Peter Elbling
Published by arrangement
with the editors
Library of Congress
Catalog Card Number:
89-91922
ISBN: 0-380-75866-0

First Avon Books Trade
Printing: December 1989

AVON TRADEMARK REG.
U.S. PAT. OFF. AND IN
OTHER COUNTRIES,
MARCA
REGISTRADA, HECHO
EN U.S.A.

Printed in the U.S.A.

BAN 10 9 8 7 6 5 4 3 2 1

Avon Books are available at special quantity discounts
for bulk purchases for sales promotions, premiums,
fund raising or educational use. Special books, or book
excerpts, can also be created to fit specific needs.

For details write or telephone the office of the Director
of Special Markets, Avon Books, Dept. FP, 105
Madison Avenue, New York, New York 10016,
212-481-5653.

CREDITS AND ACKNOWLEDGMENTS

Contributing Writers:
David Black, David Blum, Peter Cohn, Donald Fagen, Bruce Feirstein,
Lewis Grossberger, Ann Hodgman, Jeff Jarvis, Penn Jillette, Gerald Jonas,
Stefan Kanfer, Bob Mack, David Owen, Jonathan Roberts, Teller, Paul Willson.

Writers:
Kurt Anderson, Elliot Brown, George Carlin, Graydon Carter,
Graham Chapman, Jack Egan, Anthony Haden-Guest, Bruce McCall,
George Plimpton, Bob Saget, Ellis Weiner, Joshua Wesson, Jeremy Wolff.

Contributors:
Dan Barrows, Roy Blount Jr., Lloyd Carver, Tony Geiss, Carl Gottlieb, Paul Gray,
Peter Handcoff, Fayette Hickocks, Janis Hirsch, Paul Krassner, Robert Krulwich,
Philip Lazebnik, David Lander, John Leo, Lance Loud, Ann Magnuson,
Julie Payne, Margie Rocklin, Mike Wallace, Jonathan Weidman, Lotus Weinstock,
Maryann Zvoleff.

. . . .

Special Material:
Ed Begley Jr., Howard Hesseman, David Mamet, Bill Murray.

Illustrations:
Seymour Chwast, Cheri Dorr, Robert Grossman, Keith Haring,
Andrew Huffman, Elwood Smith.

Photography:
Neil Leifer, Bill Duke.

. . . .

Additional Photography: Sarah Barrett, Thomas Jackson, Keith Stapleton.
Homeless Furniture and Beast of Revelations Toy
photographed by James Rudnick.
Beast of Revelations Toy built by Sandy Forrest.
Retouching by: Robert Rakita, Ralph Wernli
Photos by: F.P.G. International, Wide World Photos Inc.,
Globe Photos Inc., Bettmann Archives, NBC Photos.
Assistant to Neil Leifer: Dan Cohen

. . . .

Special thanks to: Olga Schubart, Mel Schwartz, Janet Talley, Cinema Rentals, Kenmore Furniture.
George Spetz—Tops Appliances, John Holbrook, Jannine Agustus, Jeanne Brennan, Bill Finley,
Sharon Swenson, Don Levy, Dennis Cripps, Jeannie Wax, Ron Holder, Joe Johnson, Conversion
Limited.
Avon Books: and in particular Judith Riven.
Restaurants: Abbeylara (The Green Man), La Chaumiere, Friends of a Farmer.
People in photographs: Frank McCormack, Gary Bitterger, Luis Burgos, Edison Velez, Mario
Alvaraz, G. Schoepfer, Inc. Joshua White, Alice Playton, Steve Strassman, Patricia Stinson,
E. Darden Moorfield, Gregson Baer, Hai Chang, John Purcell, Brian Roark, Georgina McGovern,
Wolf Bashong, John L. Attanasio, John Ineir, J. Thomas, Eddie Gorodetsky, Anita Karl, Jim Kemp,
Todd Dooldridge, A. Slaughter, Larry Flannery, Thomas Jackson, Bob Mack, Mariel Hemingway,
Joe Queenan and family, Oliver Meakin, Danny Catello, Robert Keys.
Attorneys for The 90's: A Look Back: Elliot Brown, Gil Aronow (Franklin, Weinrib, Rudell, and
Vassallo).

Editor-in-Chief:
Tony Hendra
Executive Editor:
Peter Elbling

Contributing Editors:
Stephanie Brush,
Eddie Gorodetsky,
Joe Queenan,
Herb Sargent,
Paul Simms,
Rusty Unger
Editor in Absentia:
Christopher Cerf
Art Director:
Paula Scher
Associate Art Director:
Thomas Nuhn
Art Staff:
Tim Convery,
Cheri Dorr,
Ron Louie,
Kelly Walsh,
Weston Bingham,
Laurie Hinsman,
Darren Crawforth,
Laurie Henzel,
Curtis Eberhardt

AMERICA'S century ends. America's millennium begins. At least that is our hope. And the 90s have been a decade in which hope and reality have often been indistinguishable. Who's to say hope *isn't* reality if enough people believe it? The 90s have seen most people in the world finally getting what they hoped for—or at least that part of what they hoped for they could afford—or were willing to go into debt to afford. And in the 90s even those who *didn't* get what they wanted, ended up wanting what they'd got.

Who's to say the appearance of calm and peace America has enjoyed for the last ten years isn't reality? Very few major disasters have broken the surface of that tranquil pool into which we've found ourselves gazing. Or, to put this another way, if there were more than a few major disasters, we didn't know about them.

Some things we do know. We know garlic is a superconductor. We know Nostradamus' predictions that the dead would rise from their graves as the Millennium approached were true; and we have Nostradamus himself to prove it. (Not to mention the lovely and talented *Mrs.* Nostradamus.)

We know this has been called the decade of the Shortening Curve—in attention span . . . orgasm . . . nostalgia . . . cooking time.

We know this has been called the She Decade—and that having so many women in charge of so many things has brought a lot more *niceness* to everyday life.

We know this has been called the Inc. Decade, when corporations finally got the respect they'd deserved—for their size, reach, organization and ability to punish trouble-makers. For our part we've found that having only a couple of dozen really large companies around is actually easier than having hundreds of thousands. Competition may be good for executives, but for consumers it's just plain confusing.

We know all the bad diseases have been cured, or at least we think they have. And with disease, that's half the battle. We know countries seem to like one another better, those that are left anyway. And speaking of that, who's to say at the end of the day, when a disaster *is* a disaster? Long ago a wise fellow said: one man's disaster is another man's profit. Some said the Greenhouse Effect was a disaster; but if Club Meds in Iceland are bad, what's good anymore?

Did every bus in Bangladesh plunge off a cliff one day in 1996, killing the entire population of 170 million? Or was it a Wall Street joke? Disposable people make good jokes. Perhaps Bangladesh is still there, full of Bangladeshians. Who's going to go and find out?

The point is: this may not be the *real* history of the 1990s. But that doesn't matter. This is the history you *wanted*. This was the history that went down on tape and film and, very occasionally, paper. For the most part it was bright and cheery and the people were fun. Sometimes there were silly mix-ups and sometimes people got hurt, but never too badly. A good time was had by all, and all the problems got sorted out in the end. Just like life.

That's why we're finishing our century—and everyone's Millennium— not with the bang the gloomy Gusses predicted, not with the whimper the so-called intelligentsia foresaw, but with a *real feeling of accomplishment.*

Have a nice Millennium!

CONTENTS

TEHERAN 1996

THE WORLD is bigger than it was—and smaller. There are ten billion of us now; but pizza can be delivered thousands of miles in a few seconds. New countries have sprung from the ocean; others have melted. Global warming has tropicalized the tundra. Skiing and LL Bean down parkas are things of the past. But Earthlings are the same. They hustle round our world lost in wonder, searching for Eldorado, squabbling over oxygen rights. And it hardly rains anymore. Tell us this isn't still the best little planet in the whole goddam Universe.

THE WORLD

The world's most famous Mouse-oleum—
mistakenly thought by some to be a Mousque—
is a symbol of American corporate culture's majestic global sweep

THE U.S.S.R.: DAS KAPITALISM

FROM survey results given to him minutes before the 1993 Mayday Parade, Premier Gorbachev learned that 67 percent of all Russians were joggers, and 74 percent felt that quadrophonic stereo and platform shoes were essential to a "forward-looking life-style." Even more disconcerting: only 10 percent knew the premier's name.

He reflected that he only had himself to blame. *Glasnost* and *perestroika* had gotten out of hand. Drastic measures were needed to bring the country to its senses. He entered Moscow's world-renowned Museum of Art and ordered the guard to open the case containing the country's most prized treasures.

When, moments later, he took his place on the viewing stand in Red Square, the packed throng gasped in astonishment. The premier was dressed in Nikita Khrushchev's rumpled box-gray suit. Raisa blushed the color of her Halston. The premier began a lengthy diatribe against the evils of American capitalism. The crowd murmured in protest. Raising his voice, the premier reminded his countrymen that there were many good things about socialism that should not be forgotten.

"Like what?" and "Name one!" heckled the crowd. Beads of sweat appeared on the premier's forehead. "Well, there's that feeling of togetherness . . ." he began weakly. The crowd hooted in derision. Raisa rolled her eyes. The premier struggled to regain his composure. "And there's . . . Russian medical care . . ." The crowd howled. "You're acting like a schmuck," Raisa sang in his ear as she tugged violently on his sleeve. It came off in her hand. Red Square doubled over with laughter.

Fortunately, Raisa saved the day. Placing her right foot behind the premier's legs she gave him a swift elbow in the stomach which sent him tumbling off the stage. Then she seized the microphone and changed the course of history with three little words. "Let's go shopping!"

The crowd roared its approval. Chants of "RAI-SA! RAI-SA! RAI-SA!" echoed around the square. The new premier swept down the steps of the podium toward the adoring masses and then quickly marched up again so that they could admire her plunging backline.

Within weeks "mini-marts" had sprung up on every corner. American sitcoms from the seventies played around the clock and corporations were encouraged to advertise free of charge even before their products were on the shelves. Younger Soviets sipped nonalcoholic vodka, ate lo-cal caviar on English water biscuits, and discussed personal relationships in agonizing detail. Their less wealthy brethren called them Young Urban Proletarians.

They were giddy days indeed. Raisa divorced Mikhail and married Serge Topovsky, a weight lifter and part-time potato picker. Together they danced the night away at the New Old Hard Line café, where Raisa showed off her diamond-encrusted ring to anyone who asked and many who didn't.

At the same time she consolidated her power by conducting an investigation to weed out any die-hard Communists.

A redlist was quickly formed which contained over one hundred and thirty five million names. Soviet citizens lay in fear of the knock at the door, the march down to the police station, and the beady Nixonian eyes waiting for their response to the question "Are you now or have you been a member of the Communist Party?"

Husband turned in wife, brother turned in brother. Those who refused to answer were called "refuseniks" and were sent to Siberia where they were employed by Disney to build the new Trans-Siberian Thrillway.

The first person charged, found guilty, and sentenced in absentia was the former premier. Mikhail fled to the U.S. He settled in New Hampshire and spent the rest of the nineties bored to death by the ramblings of another ex-patriot, Alexander Solzhenitsyn.

In Russia, the poet, Yevtushenko, once an outspoken advocate of human rights, drew up lists of names which he recited in verse at what came to be known as the Raisa witch-hunt hearing.

A "cleaner, brighter, softer, fluffier future for all Soviet citizens," promised the new Soviet President, Raisa Gorbachev, at the first Maytag Day Parade in 1994.

Raisa solved other domestic problems with similar Western efficiency. When Afghan hordes invaded Georgia, Uzbekistan, Azerbaijan, Kazakhstan, and Tadzhikistan, which had all been clamoring for independence, she gave them their freedom. Other republics such as Latvia, Estonia, and Lithuania she sold off, claiming they were "too tacky."

On May 1, 1994, millions jammed Red Square wondering how the new regime would celebrate this now anachronistic holiday. They didn't have long to wait. The first flatbed truck carried a washer-dryer combination. The crowd responded enthusiastically. The Maytag Day Parade was underway, the revolution complete.

IT'S A DISNEY WORLD!

THIS summer—this past summer, not next summer when I'm going to spokesmodel camp if my grades are okay—I got to work for the Walt Disney Company. And it was more than an opportunity, it was an honor.

Anyway, I reported for work in June at the offices of Disneyland Classic in Anaheim. They gave me my orientation, my lie detector test (no, Todd, I *passed!*), took my blood samples, gave me my loyalty oath (which I screwed up at first!), videoed my pledge of allegiance to the flag, and I got fitted for my first character costume! I got to be the Snow White understudy. That meant that if the regular Snow White got sick Disney would let her go, and I'd take her place.

Anyway, so I did that for a week and then I found out (get this, girls) that *I was going to get to travel, free!* I got a letter personally signed by Michael Eisner himself inviting me to fly on the Disney Employee Shuttle (which my grandmother used to work for as a Flight Attendant when it was called Pan Am) to Italy, Europe, to work in the new Disney's Venice. I have the letter framed on my wall. He signs his name with little mouse ears over the *i*'s.

Disney had just bought the old Italian city of Venice and had fixed it up better than it was when it was new. Actually they had bought a whole lot of Italy, but Venice was the first part completed. They restored the old canals, and even built service tunnels underneath the city to access all the buildings for fiber optics and solid waste and stuff.

All the gondolas run on pulleys under the water like cars in a car wash so the gondoliers don't have to do anything except just stand there and make stupid comments. Oh, also 'cause Italy is a third world country they don't even have drug testing so most of the gondoliers are practically heroin addicts and I hate them.

In Venice first I sold bananas frozen and dipped in chocolate and rolled in nuts, then I portrayed Mary Poppins, then I sold churros, which is a Mexican pastry. I was best friends with these two great guys also from Orange County who portrayed Donald Doge and Mickeyavelli, two characters who had just been introduced as part of Disney's Character Acquisition Program. We had a whole lot of fun. Then the Disney people found out that one of the guys had asked me out so they sent both of them to the Disney Prison Farm in Nevada.

Then I got transferred to New York City to be part of Disney's Greenwich Village. Disney had bought this part of New York that used to be all gay people when there were a whole lot of them. It was another historic re-creation place like Venice only it was supposed to be the 1970s. All these high school and college kids were trained to portray florists and card shop owners and graphic artists and waiters and stuff. They taught us about Attitude, and how to disco dance and stuff.

My job was to portray one of these kind of men they used to have who used to portray women. They had tried using college guys for these parts, but none of them could really do it

Audio-animatronic Chairman Mickey Mao-se™ lends an ear (or two) to democratic dissenters.

Planning Center in Coeur d'Alene, Idaho, but I'm not allowed to talk about it or they'll kill my kid brother which wouldn't be so bad except for Mom and all so forget I even mentioned it.

Oh, but I *have* to tell you all about the Big Romance of the Summer. The Disney staff was very nice after the guys in Venice were sent away, and they set me up on a Disney- approved date with one of the fighter pilots in the Disney Air Force. It was fantastic. Just like "Top Gun," except he looked more like the other guy than like Tom Cruise. Oh, well.

like realistically, so then they switched and started using women. I also worked for a week at New York's Mousetropolitan Museum of Art, putting mouse ears on statues and paintings and stuff. It was sort of boring.

So I asked to get transferred, and I worked for a week in Detroit, which Disney had been hired to "clean up." I went around with a dustpan and a broom, and I was supposed to report anyone who had big radios or gold chains or Air Jordans, because they weren't allowed in anymore. I also worked for a week at the Disney World Government

We had a great time. He took me up with him one time when he buzzed Knott's Berry Farm, and another time when he strafed the Six Flags Over Texas theme park. You're going so fast that you don't see anyone get killed. It's not gross or anything.

All in all, I guess I grew up a whole lot this summer. And that's what "Dad"—Mr. Eisner —wants for America. We're all growing up along with him. I'm glad to have given this summer to the service of Disney, and mostly I just feel so much at peace since I let Mickey into my life.

Wa's Up in Japan

PACIFIC-RIM psychocultural analyst Tom Fonda Hayden-san once wrote that, given the fanatical aspect of the governing Japanese social code *Wa*, the nation was in effect a single individual. "Japan is the ultimate fascist dream," opined Hayden-san. "A hundred million plus people believing so totally in the same goals, and the same methods of achieving them, that they are their own dictator."

The American ruling right, however, moving constantly nearer to neo-Falangism, was not assuaged.

For the Podhoretz-Helms Axis, the Japanese were at once the most efficient fascists on the planet *and* the most efficient socialists. "It's just a matter of waiting out the Nipponese collectivist upstarts, and Eurocentric entrepreneurism will once again triumph," thundered the xenophobic Podhoretz in a 1992 issue of *Commentary.* "In the final analysis, they're smaller, and they're weaker. They simply don't have the staying power of Judeo-Saxons."

The Japanese, however, confounded everyone. The first community-wide inventory conducted by the EEC in 1993 concluded that 77 to 80 percent of basic cultural Euro-assets—from the real estate under national monuments to subsistence-delivery systems—were owned and operated by the Japanese. Similar studies commissioned by other geopolitical blocs (for example, the Union of Socialist South American Republics) confirmed such findings. By the mid-nineties, in all important respects Japan ruled—or at least owned—the world. They may have lost the battle—World War II—but they had incontestably won the war.

1993: The degreening of America begins. Japanese real-estate holdings (farms, vineyards, rural condo tracts) turn out to be an elaborate scheme to acquire thousands of golf courses. Entire golf courses are blasted out of their natural home and transported by dirigible across the North Pacific. Where possible they are transported to the Pacific coast, made flotational, and towed across. Anchored off Japan, American golf courses almost double the country's square mileage.

1993: The ailing CIA commissions with American industry leaders a joint study of the Japanese economic miracle. They recommend convincing the Japanese to bomb two U.S. industrial cities with small atomic bombs to stimulate new economic growth. Suggested date for the bombings is August 14, 1995. Pittsburgh and Cleveland are picked. Both cities lobby to be replaced by Detroit. (National TV campaign slogans include "Incinerate Motown" and "Nuke Detroit").

The Japanese refuse, saying they have no atomic bombs. The U.S. insists Japan spend more money on "defense." Japan counters that they are not allowed to, under their U.S.-imposed constitution. The U.S. initiates a total military blockade of Japan, lowering it only to import the latest defense technology from the "enemy." In response to the blockade, the Japanese hire the Joint Chiefs as consultants.

1994: The faces of Japanese businessmen are noticed among the regular members of Congress on C-Span TV. A short and unheralded media investigation reveals a "Congressman-for-a-Month" scheme to raise money for the ailing U.S. economy and provide wealthy Japanese with diversion.

1995: Japan Airlines expands its suborbital, supersonic transport route between Tokyo and Los Angeles—a two hour flight to the San Bernardino Valley. Crafty Californians begin taking advantage of the new service, commuting from San Bernardino to L.A. via Tokyo and beating the freeway traffic.

1995: American religions become a fad among teenagers in Japan. Coin-operated confessionals appear, and some kids become obsessed, pouring out huge amounts of money in the quest for "absolution, American-style." Perfect ecclesiastical Latin begins showing up on T-shirts and sweatshirts, taking the place of incomprehensible English word-collages. Japan acquires financial control of the Baptist faith after it goes public in the same year, and renames it the Japtist religion. American teenagers in the South, and Japanese teens at home, create an international craze for being "japtized" en masse in swimming pools.

1996: The Japanese, having long considered it a problem that there is no nice nickname for their country or people, hire Saatchi-'N Saatchi Advertising to try to "diffuse negative perceptions"—to make "Jap" and "Nip" sound acceptable, or, failing that, to come up with a better name for the nation. They try out "Nap," "Jip," "New Jap," "JapMan," and "NipMan," but nothing sticks.

1997: Japanese scientists master time travel. Technicians are sent backwards and forwards a few months, to boost past production quotas and bring back future designs of competitors.

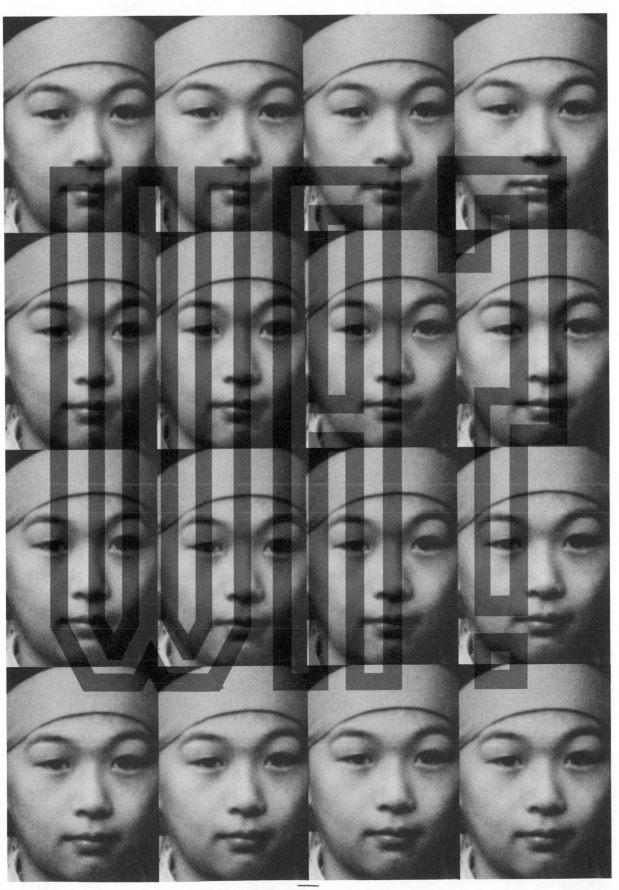

EUROPE: TO THE POWER OF TEN

MAKING the conversion was surprisingly easy. The old sixty-second minute became one hundred Euroblips equaling one Eurobite, and one hundred Eurobites of course make one Euronox.

What everybody found far harder, for some reason, was calling the timekeeping mechanism a Eurometer instead of a clock or a watch. The Germans started up that system of fines to speed the process, and that got into the whole Euroliberties debate—whether it was really quite right for the *Zeitpoleizi,* the time police, to eavesdrop on people in restaurants and parks and other places just to catch them saying *"Armbandheur,"* or wristwatch, instead of "Eurometer." That Dutch TV comedy show, the one that won the Euromirth contest, did that wonderful, wonderful segment on the Euroliberty implications of Eurotime using mime and a sundial, but by and large, people were surprisingly passive.

—Basil Runciman, Euronorth 100 (formerly London)

Eurosouth 001 is the Euronomenclatural code for Vatican City but the Roman Catholic Church still refuses to convert. The single holdout. It's something the Church of Eurosouth 100 is going to have a hard time living down.

—Giuseppi Brancati, Eurosouth 100 (formerly Rome)

My wife, Beatrix, simply could not stop weeping. At the altar at our wedding, this was. Because the Europrelate who was marrying us recited the options and she just could not understand. "Until death do us part" was too vague for the new metric world, you see, and a Eurocommittee had reformulated the marriage term into optional nuptoblips. Much more realistic in view of the divorce rate. But nonetheless, for Beatrix to be given the option of declaring her marriage vows to last for ten nuptoblips—that's ten years under the old measurement—or twenty, or thirty, and so on, was to her way of thinking terribly unsentimental for such a sentimental occasion. But she soon got over it, and we have been happily married for 6.6 nuptoblips.

—Onker Joopsma, Eurocentral 75 (formerly Leeuwarden)

I loved film as a university student and was excited to get my first job with the Eurofilm Standards Bureau on graduation. But the joy soon left me. Metrification required that every motion picture must have a running Eurotime —in the case of films, a cinedox, which is one hundred and fifty Eurobites. I was cutting down the Truffaut masterpiece *Jules and Jim* one day. I saw that it was not going to fit. That it would have to be hacked and chopped into nonsense to fit. I began to weep. They fired me for the usual antimetrification reasons. I now work as a shepherd. Killing a sheep to keep the flock at an even number is not so pleasant, but compared with the butchering of a *Jules and Jim* I must confess that I find it almost a pleasure.

—*Aloyisus Manteau, Eurocentral 80*
(formerly Lyons)

Rewriting all the popular music to metrically conform *had* to be a Eurogovernment project. Popular music is by and large about relative states of happiness. Our idea was to quantify these vague and inchoate states of feeling. This demanded incredible degrees of insight and taste on the part of the Euroeditor or Euroeditrix assigned to a particular song lyric.

There is the Gershwin song "I'll Build a Stairway to Paradise." Well! What, metrically, *is* "paradise"? It must be the ultimate—or ten. Thus, "I'll Build a Stairway to Ten." This teaches as it entertains, encouraging the listener to exchange the imprecision and folkloric connotations of "paradise" for the concrete ten. Of course, the remainder of the lyric requires adjustment to maintain a rhyming scheme. And our editors are not poets.

I cannot argue that the original lyric of "I'll build a stairway to paradise . . . with a new step every day" is phonetically more graceful than the metric version of "I'll build a stairway to ten . . . with one decimal point of increased joy each five hundred Eurobites." But metrification must go forward. As the adage goes, "Eurosouth 100 wasn't built in five hundred Eurobites."

—*Francisco Baldi, Eurosouth 90*
(formerly Milan)

The Eurobet Committee has been meeting in Eurowest 100 for six years now, trying to establish whether the old alphabet should cut down to twenty five letters or expand up to thirty. We are under terrible pressure. But one common universal Eurolingo is a goal worth sixty years—excuse me, sixty Eurodecas—to achieve. Our current inclination is for a thirty-letter Eurobet with a 10 percent option per Eurozone; that is, the German-speaking Eurozone could nominate three letters of its own, the French-speaking section its own optional three, and so forth. When and where it would be appropriate to speak or print Eurolingo using these options would be adjudicated by a Euroboard of some kind, using a weighted value system based on percentage of German- or French-speaking population within the overall Eurocommunity. But there would have to be a long-range timetable with absolutely no exceptions and one standard form of Eurolingo, by a certain distant point in Eurotime. The French support this approach, I might say. The French wish to add as one of their three optional Eurobet letters a sound, like a kiss almost. They call it the *plut.* The sound of a cigarette, or a wineglass, or other lips, leaving the lips. The emphatic *plut,* and the nuanced *plut.* So you see, if we did not have the Eurobet Committee and the Eurolingo ideal, the idea of the *plut* might have never surfaced.

—*Professor Svord Mind, Euronorth 050*
(formerly Oslo)

The metrification of addresses was a nightmare. There are six million streets in the Eurocommunity; just working out how they would be renamed according to some logical metric basis required two years of work and the founding of a whole new Euroinstitute. We finally arrived at the radial principle: the precise geographic center of Europe was determined and all street numbering relates to that. I once lived on Hansaallee 697 in Hamburg; today I live at 100–10 1.55 Street, Euronorth 40. Of course, sentiment cannot be eradicated as easily as numbers. That famous photograph of Parisians—excuse me, Eurocentral 100ers—weeping as the Champs Elysees signs came down and the Rue 25.5–500–25 signs went up—will haunt the Euromemory for a long Eurotime to come.

—*Francis Rhoem, Euronorth 40*
(formerly Hamburg)

THE RESTORATION OF KING CHARLES III

THE incoming Socialist government of March 1992 was eager. Disregarding warnings from such allies as President Mitterand, they began dismantling the Thatcherite Revolution in a rush. It was when they disarmed the British forces that the Iron Lady struck.

Her actual seizure of power was accomplished with little bloodshed (the Minister of Aviation accidentally fell from his office window and a few junior members of Parliament perished while "helping the police with their inquiries"). And the fickle electorate had only voted the Socialists in because Labor leader Neil Kinnock had undergone a sex change, leaving him with a startling resemblance to Mrs. Thatcher. They were quickly getting bored with Labor and thought the whole thing was a bit of a lark. They agreed, by and large, that the country needed "a bit of stick," and the swoop by Special Branch on the intelligentsia, letter-writers to the *Independent,* etc. etc., which was followed by their detention at a tent city in North London (Gulag NW5, as it was soon known), generated a tremendous wave of popular enthusiasm.

Thatcher's First Hundred Days were a triumph, as one at a time she ticked items off her political shopping list. Its milestones were:

The "privatization" of the National Health Service, by handing it over to the highest bidder, Dow Chemical.

The acquisition of the BBC by Rupert (Lord) Murdoch.

The reassignment of the wishy-washy Church of England to "tougher" pastoral duties. The Archbishop of Canterbury was reassigned to the Thatcher Islands (formerly the Falklands).

A "pill tax" levied on every pill consumed in the United Kingdom.

A "pall tax" levied on everyone who actuarially could be expected to die within the next century.

A "peel tax" levied on every piece of fruit consumed in the United Kingdom.

A "pal tax" levied on everyone in the United Kingdom who had a friend.

As the eventful weeks passed, attention began to focus on the Leader's only rival. Nothing had been heard from the Queen—always a stickler for constitutional propriety. But when Mrs. Thatcher formed—or rather appointed—her own Parliament, no monarch was present at its Opening. In retaliation the Iron Lady put the Life Guards and the Blues under the direct command of the incoming Minister of Tourism, Robin Leach, and the royal temper exploded.

The two finally met publicly in July. The place was the paddock at Ascot and it is possible that hostilities could have been avoided but the Duke of Edinburgh hot-bloodedly took a riding crop to the Minister of Culture, Jeffrey Archer. When Mrs. Thatcher tried to intervene the Queen prevented her, insisting that she curtsy in the royal presence. Mrs. Thatcher refused. The Queen then ripped the Leader's expensive hat from her head and trod it into

COMMEMORATIVE

E II R

14ᴾ

The beheading of the royal couple in the tower of London on that cloudless Monday morning was noted for its "typical British pageantry" and the tasteful TV coverage.

the mud, calling her adversary "a bluenosed loudmouthed grammar-school bully" and "a bloodless, heartless, witless, tasteless tart."

The subsequent beheading of the royal couple in the Tower of London on that cloudless Monday morning was noted for its "typical British pageantry" and the tasteful TV coverage. (The Queen was looking "radiant in black velvet," according to Barbara Walters, who later did a prime-time human-interest interview with the executioner). But many thought that Mrs. Thatcher was going too far when she announced that she now wished to be known by a title not used since the late Oliver Cromwell: the Protector.

Even so, the first summer of the Protectorate was a heady one. Merger makers, defense contractors, Mormons, and televangelists flooded in from the U.S. accompanied by arbitrageurs, postmodernist architects, and interior decorators specializing in *le style Rothschild*. St. Paul's Cathedral was razed to make way for luxury flats to accommodate the neo-Roundheads. Joan Collins announced that she would be starring as Mrs. Thatcher in a thirteen-part series (despite the Protector's stated preference for Lee Remick).

Things began to darken in the fall. Too late, the Protector began to realize that she had been rash to allow the junior royals to flee into exile in the EEC. Her steely supposition that ten years of Silly Gossip Coverage had made them harmless was wide of the mark. Dissident elements began to flock around the royal standard of their choice, with acting and dance professionals swearing fealty to Prince Edward while numerous ex-servicemen and automobile-parts calendar girls offered their support to Prince Andrew.

But it was "Bonnie" Prince Charles who at-

tracted the broadest spectrum of support, ranging from CAMRA to SDPers to ultratraditional aristos and even neo-Luddites.

Global opinion now made it impossible for the Protector to crush the "King Across the Water" openly, so covert countermeasures were tried. Thatcherite foes began meeting with curious accidents. An alleged vagrant doused Harold Pinter with meths, and tried to set him alight. David Hockney was found floating in his California pool. Vanessa Redgrave succumbed to a poisoned bagel. Then a squad of supposed animal-rights activists tried to kidnap Princess Anne. They were beaten off by a platoon of soccer hooligans, who came to the defense of the Crown, apparently under the impression that it was a pub.

The tide began to turn. As the U.S. government retreated into a miasma of unreality, Thatcher's parasitic economy shriveled and died. Shorn of wealth, the full dowdiness of her Protectorate became clear to the British people—and not the least because their traditional escape route to romance and exotica, Europe, was denied them. Yuppies sickened on the urinelike wines brewed by entrepreneurs in Hampshire and Kent; businessmen brought to sexual frenzy by lack of contact with their French and Italian mistresses caused appalling carnage on the motorways.

Ironically it was Charles, exiled in Paris, who was the beneficiary of British disillusion with Thatcherism. Despite his Earth shoes and love of whales, King Chuck, as the tabloids were calling him, became a romantic hero. Divorced from Di, he was rumored to be having it off with whatever bit of Euroskirt caught his fancy; his adroit financial moves (he went personally public in 1995) compared favorably with the debt- and foreclosure-ridden mess the Lady Protector had bequeathed her people.

Good King Charles enjoys a pint at his favorite pub,
The Crown in Bayswater. The popular monarch is known affectionately as King Chuck the Equal.

The end was swift. On April 23, 1996, Charles, supported by the full might of the EEC defense forces, removed the barricades at the Normandy end of the Chunnel (placed there by the French upon its completion in 1993). At the other end of the tunnel, he "opened the door to England" to an ecstatic greeting by millions of his subjects, who were desperate for sex, sunshine, untaxed alcohol, and lard-free food.

The Iron Lady Protector went bravely to her death. All in all her execution was tastefully arranged. She was permitted to return to No. 10 Downing Street, but for once security forces had not swept the surrounding housetops or dismantled the usual bombs. For the IRA of course, unaware of any political developments in the UK other than those which directly involved them, it was a day like any other. With one difference. That night, they too had something to celebrate.

PALES
chic

ROCCO LANDESMAN and The First National West Bank of Palestine PRESENTS

Judd **HIRSCH** in:

A Sizzling Musical Comedy

YASIR,
He's My Baby!

The Music of Palestinian Liberation!

Bernadette **PETERS** as *Mrs. Arafat*

Ed **ASNER** as *Ariel Sharon*

and featuring the music of **The Palestinian Light Orchestra**

at the **JUJAMCYN THEATER, 555 West 54th St.**

Judd Hirsch knocked 'em dead with his show-stopping torch song "(I'm Just A) Hostage Of Love."

TINIAN

The flagship of Palestine's airline offers seating in First, Coach and Imperialist Dog classes.

World leaders confer at the Beirut Economic Summit before sitting down to a delicious meal of stewed goat eyes served on a pile of rice on the floor.

TORAH, TORAH, TORAH!

THE Old Order crumbled on January 19, 1992. Menachem Begin stepped onto his balcony after many years of seclusion. He was no longer bald and jaundiced, but was robust of stature, with a majestic white mane flowing down over long robes (surprising many in the intelligence community who had assumed he was dead). Begin declared, "I have thought long and hard during these years of isolation. I have come to understand one thing. I am not a Jew." And with that he held up an ancient scroll, later termed The New Talmud, The Book of Those and Those Who are Not. It revealed to the world that the following are not Jews:

• Those who are Men who have received more than fifty shekels upon their thirteenth year.

• Those who are Women who have sought to alter the form given unto them by the Lord, be it through fasting or movements that are of unnatural burden or duration.

• Those whose hands have entered the mouth of another and have built bridges therein, just as it is so of those who have severed, removed, or exchanged the organs that lie within the body.

• Those who have sought to present Spectacle, Fancy, Amusement, or Diversion in any and all media in any territory, foreign or domestic.

• Those who have dwelt (or falsely stated the hope of dwelling) in the territory beyond the Jordan, bounded on the south in the valley opposite Bethpeor and on the north by Mount Hermon, the edge of the valley of Arnon, and all those who have suffered trees to be planted thereon or purchased stock, bonds, or other debt securities.

The paradox at the heart of the Who-is-a-Jew controversy could not have been more sharply dramatized. Only the most Jewish of Jews could be relied upon by other Jews to define Jewishness out of existence.

Me-too renunciations followed by the millions. Accusations and counteraccusations were everywhere. Those who streamed out of Israel in the following months to less economically devastated territories like Beirut or Ethiopia were regarded as reneging on their obligations to the homeland. But as many pointed out, if they had felt an obligation to Israel they were no longer Jewish, so how could they now have an obligation to Israel?

In the United States the results were equally dramatic. No situation comedies were produced in Los Angeles in the 1992–93 season.

Caries and cavities became the number one health problem. The Security Council passed a passionate resolution on December 14, 1992, declaring not just that Israel had a right to exist, but that it *must* exist. Without Israel, it concluded, the Security Council had no reason to exist.

But no institution was as shaken as was the *New York Times*. It shrank within days after Begin's proclamation to two sections, then one. For the first four months of 1993 the paper carried no department store, supermarket, theater, or financial services advertising. The Sunday edition was buried beneath an avalanche of self-decimating think pieces from its regular contributors. Then the paper ceased publication altogether.

When the *Times* returned it was a much-changed and chastened paper. Many names had disappeared, notably those at the top of the masthead, which was now graced by a stately family of Schultz-Burghers. The new editor in chief was Dipth Pran. Most important, Page Three of the first section, traditional home of "Mideast" news, carried a five-column ad for Pizza Hut and a story on the health hazards of smoked fish.

But one man stood against the flood of de-semitization, the *Times* Tel-Aviv bureau chief Morton Arthur. Ignored by his paper, Arthur filed regular stories over the next four years, all of them increasingly hopeless. Here is his last:

Can you Ignorami remember what it used to be like? War. Shuttle Diplomacy. Superpowers. Blonde Olive-Skinned Hitchhikers in Tight-Fitting Army Shorts. Stonings. Terror. Injustice. Ambiguity. Hopelessness. It was bliss, for it was news.

Sometimes it was front-page news and that was soaringly wonderful because there was my name. But no matter what day it was, it was a News Day in Israel. The Hole had to be filled. Because this was the *New York Times*, and Mort

was their man, and *they* were the people that ran it, just as *they* were the people who read it and shopped at Bloomingdale's and voted for Republicans and gave money to Democrats. And Mort would feed their hole. The Pulitzer was in his grasp.

And then came the day when He gave us the Scrolls. The birth of the UnJews. The Deconversion. And for Mort, Soul Death. Nonbeing, nontology. Mort was out of a job.

But Mort believed he was still a Jew and a teller of stories. Mort still had his laptop, his fax, his Nikon. Deny thyself, said he. Rise up, rise up. File thy dispatches. What would work?

He tried food. Seventeen creative recipes using milk and honey. Nothing.

He tried a think piece. A call for a return to the angst-ridden post-Vietnam incompetence of the 70s or the Evangelical Phallus-oriented gunboat diplomacy of the 80s. Nothing.

The ideas cascaded. Establish a Palestinian Homeroom. Issue hall passes, gold stars, demerits, that kind of thing. Nothing.

Then Mort found news, legitimate news. A new group in the land, a new power. Zealots calling themselves Jews Who Used to Be Jews Who Are Also for Jesus (the Christian Zionists) have established a kibbutz and waterskiing clinic (in case they are driven into the sea). Nothing.

And now the ultimate. A new Christ has arisen in the desert. The Second Coming, he says. The Masadists, the only Ones left, the diehards, those who condemned Begin not as a prophet but as wimpy, left-wing compromiser took the new Christ, tried him and recrucified him. And three days later he rose from the dead. And it's all on videotape.

Still nothing.

So damn you, Gray Lady. Mort's leaving too. Mort's going to Milan to marry a Catholic and start a clothing firm called DeZion Associates. Mort is a Jew no more.

In Nineteen Hundred and Ninety Two...

*Excerpts from the transcript of "Big" Tony Taglio's testimony in Tokyo, Japan, where he was arraigned
on charges of grand theft, assault and battery, piracy on the high seas,
murder, and cannibalism*

IT was after bowling, me an' Vinnie, Louie, Mike, Billy, Paulie, about twen'y a us was eatin' pizza, an' Louie says he seen this TV show where the Nips were gonna... *domo,* yer honor, *domo,* the Japanese was gonna do Columbus' five-hundredth anniversary voyage. An he's all pissed off aboudit. He says, "If Columbus was Italian, how come it's bein' done by the Nips?" *domo,* yer honor, *domo.*

Anyways, Louie gets one a his macho spasms. He jumps on a table an' he says, "Kennedy's just roun' the fuckin' corner, fer crissake! Let's go over there an' show 'em." So, to humor him, we goes down to Kennedy airport. I'm thinkin' this is all a game—I mean, we still got our bowlin' shit an' everythin'. But then Vinnie's always gotta show how his dick's bigger than Louie's, he buys a ticket. Half hour later I'm on a fuckin' plane to Spain!

I don' remember how we got to Cadiz. Maybe we took a cab. Anyways there they are. The *Nina 2,* the *Pinta 2,* an' the *Santa Maria 2.* Now I seen 'em I wanna go home, but Paulie says we gotta go on board.... Why didn't I object, yer honor? You get tapped on the head widda bowling ball, you go.

Inside the *Santa Maria* it looked like somebody thieved a Sony warehouse. This fuckin' boat coulda gone to the moon. Computers, radar, sonar, the works. But I says, I mean *Vinnie* says, If Columbus made the voyage widout all this shit, the Japs should do widout it, too. So we threw it overboard...

Then Matty, he's on the *Nina,* he shouts, "Race alla youse across the harbor." He wants to race—no problem. By now the coastguards are goin' apeshit. Then some jerk wid a hard-on fires a shot right in fron' a us. So, Paulie puts a bowlin' ball inna cannon an' BOOM! Blew a hole in that sonofabitch the size a the fuckin' Lincoln Tunnel. I thought, That's it, it's all over, my ass is grass, but this fog comes down, covers everythin'. You couldn't see yer hand in fron' a yer face. An' when it lifts up the coastguards are gone, the harbor's gone, an' the *Pinta*'s gone. An' we're in the middle a the fuckin' ocean. Lost.

So I says, "Hey, we're Americans, right? We don' back down. No way, no how. We come this far. Let's go fer it. Let's go find a new fuckin' world." Well, the guys start goin' "Awright! Awright!" I mean, it was beautifu'. Like when we almost won the league in seventy-two. We was a team. Mike, he's on the *Pinta,* he wants to follow the sun, Eddie says we gotta steer by the stars. You ever seen how many stars are out there? Meantime, the wind is blowin' us roun' an' roun' in circles an' Paulie's goin' on about how we gotta be in tune wid the elements.

Three weeks later we're outta food, we're freezin' our tits off, an' the guys on the *Nina* are mutinizin'. They're blamin' me. Like it was my fuckin' idea to go to the South Pole. So one word leads to another an' the next thing I know we're havin' a regular war out in the middle a nowhere. They're firing bowlin' balls at us an' threatenin' to kick our asses from one end a the Atlantic to the other. I says to Vinnie, "This is bullshit," an' we steer the *Santa Maria* right into the *Pinta* an' down she goes. Then we change course. East, west, I dunno.

Now it's two months. . . . we're eating belts, shoes, ropes. Wood. Anythin' I can get in my mouth I'm eatin'. Then Eddie starts sayin' how cute I am. I says, "Listen, you try somethin', asshole, I'll cut yer fuckin' balls off." So what happens? He comes at me. I cut his balls off, an' I ate 'em. . . . What was I supposed to do?

One by one the guys buy the farm an' then it's just down to me an' Vinnie. We're standin' in the middle of the boat about to fight to the death an' see who gets to eat who, when I look up, an' I swear on my mudder's grave, I see land. Not just land, but a moun'in. A goddamn moun'in.

We fall down on our knees an' kiss the ground. Then I notice something funny. I gotta mouthful a coffee grinds. The land is garbage. All garbage. A moun'in a garbage! We start walkin'. It goes on fer miles. We walked three weeks an' we didn't get nowhere. There's a whole fuckin' continent a garbage out in the middle a the ocean.

So we called it Garbantis, an' we claimed it fer Italy. Oh, sure, yer honor, we coulda claimed it fer Japan. There's a lotta yer stuff in there, believe me. But the point is, *we* did it! Nineteen hundred and ninety two, we set out to sail the ocean blue. And we discovered a New World!

Just so happens, it's a pile a garbage.

AMERICA THE BEAUTIFUL people God shed his grace on you! Some have called you "the tyranny of celebrity" and a "dictatorship of the shirking classes." One ingrate even dubbed you "face-ists." Well we say pooh to that! Beautiful America brings us non-stop fun, excitement, and heart-warming personal triumphs. It allows us to share the hopes and fears and loves of people so rich and gorgeous we could never dream of being like them. And that's what makes America beautiful.

FINALLY—
YOU CAN
BE
SOMEBODY
ELSE!

HIGH
TOPIARY

F.I.R.M.
(THE
FACIALLY
IMPAIRED
RIGHTS
MOVEMENT)

WHITE
NIGHTS,
BLACK
CITY

THE
CENTRAL
PARK PASS
LAW

GUARD MY
BODY, BIG
GUY

THE
TRAGEDY
OF THE
SECOND-
HOMELESS

A
HARDENING
OF THE
ARTS

HIZZONER!
WILLIAM
MURRAY,
MAYOR OF
CHICAGO

WHERE
ARE THEY
NOW?

AMERICA THE BEAUTIFUL

Ms. Meryl Streep, co-chairperson of the Coalition for the Nasally Impaired.

FINALLY—YOU CAN BE SOMEBODY ELSE!

SAID Ulrike Schnirre, fashion-model-turned-body-entrepreneur, in 1993: "A woman can have a variety of 'body-looks' when she's clothed—she should also, when naked, have this same ability."

During the nineties, cosmetic surgery finally jumped the gap we all knew it needed to. From "elective" to "compulsory."

Due to the pioneering work of Cher, Phyllis Diller, and Dick Clark, plastic surgery even became recognized as a physical *addiction*—an addiction, interestingly, for both the patients undergoing the surgery and the doctors performing it.

Plastic surgery "junkies" began to disdainfully refer to the bodies they were originally born with as their "birth bodies."

Or as Avram Nasturtium of the American Society of Whole-Body Cosmetic Surgeons put it: "Holding on to the body you were 'born' with is like buying a house and deciding to live with the previous owner's wallpaper."

The plastic-surgery watchwords of the 90s —and there were many—were "convenience," "flexibility," and "reversibility."

If the 80s had essentially been represented by removable shoulder *pads,* the 90s spoke to the need for removable *shoulders.*

From Mel 'n Michele's body styling drive-in franchise in a suburban Chicago mall ($599 for this week's special, a jiffy neck elongation), to Manhattan's sleak forty-seven-story House of Fashions in Flesh ($999,000 for a skeletal transplant to tauten the skin), business boomed. On the eve of a new century, anatomy was no longer destiny.

The "self-service surgery" movement also took America by storm, particularly with the introduction of Velcroderm™. At last, a method of circumventing messy "incisions"— you could simply flip open a patented, Velcro-like flap of skin and insert the breast or other implant, in any size of your choice. Or remove it, if you wanted a more "man-tailored" breast look.

The most wildly popular fad, among teens, was inarguably "self-service liposuction." ("Just like people finally got tired of having to sit at a gas station back in the seventies, waiting for some lazy drug-crazed attendant to come out and wait on them . . . you know?" said one teenage owner of a popular chain of self-liposuction franchises.)

A customer could simply position a small vacuum hose between his or her lips, adjust

Trimming down thighs and fannies with a quick suck became a must-do part of morning and evening make-overs.

Plastic surgeons made millions off the "Celebrity Look." In the fall of '95, a face-ectomy and a Hoffmanoplasty or a Brinkleyplasty were the operations to get.

the controls, and siphon out unwanted fat from a variety of body areas. "You'll wonder where the Jell-O went," cooed Revlon.

Sometimes a self-liposuction customer accidentally swallowed his or her own fat, making it necessary to undergo the whole process again. (But as with tanning salons, the dangers were comfortingly and fancifully underrepresented or falsified.)

On a facial plane, one disturbing trend was that, grappling with unlimited "beauty freedom of choice," several hundred thousand Americans woke one morning in 1996 as Tom Cruise.

By 1995, you could visit any computer-surgery outlet and buy a computer grid which would automatically "stamp out" your favorite celebrity's likeness on you (using a thousand tiny "contact points," much as a VCR "copies" a game show)—all on an outpatient basis!

Creative Artists Agency, representing Brooke Shields, Vanna White, Michele Pfeiffer, Tom Cruise, Mel Gibson and many others sued IBM and Apple in a landmark case which gave celebrities the power to copyright their features.

The sociological changes wrought by the PE (Personal Enhancement) explosion have yet to be assessed. Arguments abound, with conservatives insisting that society benefits by an easily recognizable economic class division in which the poor are old and ugly and the rich are young and beautiful—"survival of the prettiest." The counterconservative Right-to-Knife movement has waged a political battle to make aesthetic surgery available to all (as in Sweden), a part of every citizen's inalienable right to the pursuit of happiness ("and beauty," as they would have the Constitution amended).

Splinter groups like the tiny radical "Free to Be Wee" contingent hold demonstrations outside PE clinics to protest certain aesthetic tenets of PE, such as the fashion for enormous breasts and penises.

HIGH TOPIARY—
THE BLACK HAIRSTYLES
OF THE 90s

High Topiary reached its peak in 1990 when the combined hairstyles of three Brooklyn teenagers fit together to form the continent of Africa. Unfortunately, Jerome (Sahara and the north) caught Shortstuff (Equatorial Africa) putting the make on his girl, Kendra (Angola, Namibia and Zimbabwe) dividing the country irrevocably.

F.I.R.M.

"**THE** most insidious form of discrimination practiced by Hollywood is prejudice against the facially impaired. For too long butt-ugly Americans have been denied their right to a full rich life, and we more than anyone are to blame." Thus read the opening sentences of the most controversial document of the decade, the Facially Impaired Rights Manifesto. For a few months in 1994, it ignited a movement that changed not just the way celebrities thought, but the way they looked.

Some—like Darryl Hannah and Barbra Streisand of the West Coast IRS (Immensely Rich Socialists)—were so inspired they voluntarily underwent surgery to become one with the butt-ugly. "It was beautiful," said one facially impaired fan, "these beautiful people giving up their own *beauty* to identify with the butt-ugly."

BARBRA STREISAND

HARRISON FORD

ROBERT DENIRO

GRACE JONES

WHITE NIGHTS, BLACK CITY

ON a balmy moonlit evening in September 1996, Jay McInerney's Great Black and White Ball commenced in Central Park. By every account it was due to be the single most glittering social event of the decade.

Workmen had toiled for weeks to erect a tent over almost the entire park—from 59th to 102nd Streets. Scheduled events included a 10K black-tie run around the reservoir and sodium-lit polo in the Sheep Meadow.

"It just made so much sense to do it in Central Park," said professional party-giver Mai Hallingby, munching on white truffles and black caviar in a sky box high above the Trump carousel. "After all, nasty old Mr. Greenhouse has already turned the grass white and the trees black. The whole thing was pre—color-coordinated." Added her partner in "Parties Mondiales" Misha Baryshnikov, "And it's really great that Jay's not charging admission."

(Charity functions had become so all-pervasive by 1996 that socialites routinely charged as much as a thousand dollars merely to have lunch. Even simple phone calls cost upward of two hundred and fifty dollars. Five hundred dollars if they were returned.)

Among the first arrivals was Liz Smith, fresh from a launching party for her new magazine *Smith's* at the Trump-Puck Building.

Smith said she was even more pleased with the launch earlier in the week of her new fragrance "Liz" at Trumpingdale's. "Now I'm *really* nineties," quipped Liz. "I have a magazine *and* a fragrance."

By ten o'clock things were in full swing. John Fairchild ("Man" the fragrance, *Fairchild* the magazine) chatted amiably with Clay Felker ("Clay," *Felker's*) and former *Spy* editor E. Graydon Carter ("E.," *Carter's*). (Fairchild purchased *Spy* in 1992, installed Felker as editor, and spun off a tabloid for hardcore *Spy* readers called *Spite*.) The two were congratulating Carter on his recent acquisition of Celebrity Service and his first annual "E. Graydon Carter/Earl Blackwell Ten Best-Dressed list."

"There are only two great sports left in the nineties," mused veteran phrase-maker Carter as he gazed out over the Sheep Meadow polo grounds, where well-known surgeons and lawyers flailed at each other's ponies. "Litigation and elective surgery." Carter's own trial for "excessive use of pejoratives with criminal intent" had of course recently ended in acquittal.

After a triumphant world tour, the Berlin Wall finds a permanent home in another divided city, New York.

When pressed by a reporter on the subject Carter reddened and replied, "Get outta here, you short-fingered churlish dwarf-like former author or I'll adjective you to death."

Nearby, Normal Mailer ("Ego,"*Mine*) discussed plans for a new book on the late Madonna with Teamster president Curtis Sliwa ("Mace,"*Sliwa's*) and Stephen Sprouse ("Again?," *S.S.*), CEO of the "Limited Gap J. Crew" Retail Corp. The aging Mailer was primed for a fight with all comers, but celebrated art-murderer Richard ("When sculpture falls on someone and kills them it's part of the conception") Serra literally beat him to the punch. Serra was subsequently decked by Julian Schnabel whose work had also recently killed work-men during installation. "Only one guy died?" bellowed the con-temptuous Schnabel. "For art to be great it must kill dozens, scores, hundreds!"

The high point of the evening came when Jay himself arrived, escorted by Donald and Ivana Trump. Jay was dressed in two fabulous white silk shirts. "I have several thousand of them," he told his date, Athina Onassis. "They're so beauti-ful I could cry," said Athina. And she did.

Elsewhere Larry Tisch, and Paulina Porizkova discussed their up-coming honeymoon, which was to end so tragically; Henry Kravis and Andie MacDowell nuzzled with their baby pictures; ditto Saul Steinberg and Rachel Williams. Even Carl Bernstein ("Ink," *Red Diaper*) was there with bride-to-be Carolyn Mossbacher and Cornelia Guest Paley, still grieving over the loss of her beloved Bill.

Many Kennedys were present as usual. Al-most all were excitedly discussing the recent Kennedy convention at the Kennedy Conven-tion Center in Hyannisport, where patriarch

Ted had announced the family's goal for the twenty-first century—one million Kennedys by 2050 A.D. "I'm game," said impish Caroline Kennedy, eyeing recently estranged Shriver spouse, Arnold Schwarzenegger.

White—the color of happiness and light—was the theme of the evening. But shades of black were evident too. East Village real estate tycoon Michael Musto ("Must," *Beneath the Village Voice*) had just come from the funeral of restaurateur Glenn Birnbaum, who had been killed the day before when a group of upper-middle-echelon MBAs went "wilding" in his empty restaurant, Mortimer's, after being told no tables were available.

Others, like Kelly Klein, were in a philosophical mood. "It's a pity we'll never be young again," said the former Mrs. Calvin Klein. "Yes," replied Cindy Lauper von Bulow, "but at least we'll never be poor."

Finally long after the last polo pony had been led away and the last jar of beluga had been slipped into the last handbag, Jay himself rose from the table near the boathouse where he had been holding court. As the sun gilded the soaring towers of Zuckerman Circle, he stepped into the *gondola* of the Whittle Blimp, resplendent with ads for magazines and fragrances, and made the short trip to the northernmost boundary of *his* party, the 102nd Street pedestrian transfer. There, with a flourish of white silk he pressed a remote control and the entire north wall of the Great Tent fell away, revealing his gift to his friends, and to his beloved city.

Running from Central Park West to Fifth Avenue clear across the park, fresh from its triumphant world tour, was a half-mile section of the Berlin Wall. Jay's cheering guests immediately dubbed it the Great Black and White Wall. To this day that is how it's known, the ultimate symbol of a New York spirit that would not be cowed, and of a light of wit and style that would not be dimmed.

THE CENTRAL PARK PASS LAWS

AFTER a series of assaults on male and female joggers in northern Central Park, Pass Laws became the number-one topic in New York City. Most commentators agreed that in 102 out of 107 incidents, the attackers tended to be of one hue and the joggers of another. At the convention of Retail Crack Dealers in Panama City, talk-show host William Kunstler disagreed.

He reminded his enthusiastic audience that the perpetrators were the "inevitable results of the 1989 Supreme Court decision against abortion on demand."

Eventually, the Pass Laws went into effect in 1997, after a visiting Australian talk-show host was slain and served with mint sauce in the Sheep Meadow. The laws stated that nonwhite persons in "felony shoes," or high-top sneakers, had to carry pass books when in Central Park and could not stay in the park for more than twenty minutes unless they resided there since birth or were licensed bird watchers.

Through 1997–98, 508,641 persons were arrested for violation of the Pass Laws, and were filtered through special courts. Trials rarely lasted more than thirty seconds, and many were held in the revolving doors in the lobby of the criminal courts normally used to try murderers and former members of the National Security Council. Conviction brought flogging or, in extreme cases, a fine. Both were vigorously protested by senators and congressmen with residences outside the city. In the most famous demonstration, virtually every person of Third-World ancestry under the age of twenty-one called for sanctions against the park. In some two million leaflets airdropped over the city, talk-show host Ivana Trump countered that "if we all stop patronizing Tavern on the Green, it's the poor who will suffer most." Despite this barrage, a boycott was enforced primarily by the United Brotherhood of Feral Gangs Local 1. For six months, in the spring and summer of 1999, not one governor, mayor, congressman, talk-show host, or nonwhite under the age of twenty-one entered Central Park. During that period the crime rate fell by 99.7 percent.

Coincidentally, the number of assaults on male and female professionals in the Wall Street area *rose* during the same period by exactly the same percentile.

GUARD MY BODY, BIG GUY

PICTURE the biggest kid in your school. You try to avoid trouble but when it comes knocking—you open the door with a smile. You kinda dig it. You like the fast lane, show biz, glamour, money—and face it, you think you look good in the horns. You're a born Motherfucker™.

And if you make it, kid, you'll be proud. It's a field as old as history and as modern as the newest subminiature fully automatic hand-nuke.

If you want to know who the Boss M.F. looks up to, it's "Big Chick" Huntsberry. He gave me my career.

February 17, 1992. I was in this bar and I had a load on. The Grammies were on the tube. That skinny little faggot, Prince, won something and got up with his bodyguard, "Big Chick." This one asshole in the bar said that "Big Chick" was probably muscle-bound and Prince just kept him around so that he could bang him. Two hours later I was in the drunk tank with his blood all over my pants. I decided that night to be the toughest bodyguard around.

Then fate stepped in. I don't know what Dick Cavett was doing in Central Park at that hour but he was crazy enough to think that tae kwon do was going to protect his spindly ass from the teenage wolf pack. (That was the first week that deaths in the park were in the double digits.) Personally, I think he was just looking for the press. And me killing three of the assholes got him plenty.

Dick and I did the whole talk-show circuit. Dick kept trying to call me his "Urban Samurai" but the press picked up on what I had called myself—"just one tough motherfucker." No one had bothered to copyright the word *motherfucker* but my newfound lawyer did it fast enough. By the end of the year I had two dozen Motherfuckers™—elite steroid-enhanced bodyguards prepared to administer deadly force. Soon Dick Cavett was working for *me*. He was our spokesman and our model. He also did some work around my apartment.

If Dick had weighed more than a hundred pounds I probably never would have gotten the idea to carry him around on my back. It turned out to be real practical. I always knew where my "papoose" was.

Celebrities loved the idea. Then some smart-ass newspaper cartoonist drew my pic-

"Step aside, citizen." The Motherfucker is nothing if not polite.

ture with a papoose and horns and I liked the way that looked too. By spring 1992, Motherfucker™ Inc. had become the number-one celebrity protection service in the country.

Of course I was the brunt of a few jokes. It really braised my chicken when Letterman did his Top Six Things Overheard at a Motherfucker Training Session.

1. "That's *Mister* Motherfucker."

2. "I heard Demi Moore likes to ride facing backwards."

3. "My nightmare is failing the written test and getting stuck with Dom Deluise."

4. "Is that a bone graft or are you just happy to see me?"

5. "He's a really nice guy. He'd give you the hair off his back."

6. "It's not a *literal* term. She's sixty-three years old."

Of course Letterman got roughed up in front of 30 Rockefeller Center. And I had the last laugh. He hired his own Motherfucker™.

THE TRAGEDY OF THE SECOND-HOMELESS

THEY started appearing shortly after George Bush's first inauguration—in Southampton, in Lenox, in Booth Bay Harbor—with their L.L. Bean tents, the Coleman stoves, the shopping bags filled with provisions from Balducci's and Zabar's.

The second-homeless.

There were only a few at first, strolling along the streets, gazing into shop windows as if they really were considering buying that Guatemalan hammock for the veranda of the beach house they wanted us to believe they owned.

We recognized them as interlopers by the all-too-ingratiating neighbor-to-neighbor smiles they gave us; and, when there were only two or three of them in the community, their feverish, eager desire to fit in was touching. It made us want to reach out and offer, if not our guest cottages, at least our beachfronts riding rings or gazebos, someplace private enough for them to seek shelter and maintain a scrap of dignity.

They were, for the most part, hardworking, respectable members of their own communities. But through socioeconomic circumstances that had trapped them in generations of second-homelessness, they had never been able to escape from the tragic cycle, which doomed them to a mean existence of owning—or, worse, renting—just one home.

By the time the second-homeless began appearing in greater numbers, two and three to every street corner, some of the more conservative members of our community wanted to take strong measures. To have police sweeps that would overcrowd our small town jails. To commit them to state mental hospitals for observation—for, as one of my neighbors said, "They must be crazy to come all the way to the Hamptons or the Berkshires just to sleep in the open, without air-conditioning."

Some of the more generous among my neighbors organized Evian-lines and bisque kitchens in church basements for the unfortunates, who, after a weekend in the hot summer sun, could not possibly have any fresh lox left.

The incident that started the vigilantism was innocuous. On the hottest day of 1992, a second-homeless man in Cape May, New Jersey, paused to bathe his face in the sprinkler that was watering John Henry Kurtz's front lawn.

Kurtz appeared in his doorway, naked from the waist up. Strapped to his hips was a brace of 1860 Colt Army cap-and-ball revolvers from his legendary collection of Civil War memorabilia. Kurtz blasted away at the intruder, who escaped uninjured but left behind a bag of practically untouched eclairs from Dumas Patisserie.

Other similar vigilante incidents brought retaliation from the second-homeless—like dropping Dove Bar wrappers in driveways and cutting in line at some movie theaters. The tragic cycle of violence then escalated, as signs began appearing, first in boutiques, then in sporting-goods stores and restaurants: NO PETS AND SECOND-HOMELESS ALLOWED. Fistfights disrupted quiche-lines in Hyannisport. Throughout August 1992 it was impossible to get reservations at the Red Lion Inn in Stockbridge because the second-homeless organized brunch-ins. Children of the second-homed broke their vacation house keys in sympathy.

Across the nation, states passed legislation forbidding the second-homeless from entering what were designated as *resort sectors*. The response was immediate and explosive: the second-homeless—who were, after all, the majority—organized to run their own candidates in the '94 elections. Congress, solidly second-homed, whether on the right or the left, united in the face of the threat. Legislation was proposed that would limit the right to vote to citizens with at least two properties. "The

After spending the off-season as squatters in a mansion on the Vineyard, a second-homeless family begs politely for help.

Founders gave the vote to people of property," opined Chief Justice Rehnquist at his summer place on the Chesapeake. "Besides, the selective principle implied means we must distinguish between the Toms, Dicks, and Harrys with one heavily mortgaged piece of ticky-tacky and those of us who've got our mitts on some substantial pieces of real estate."

In any event, the legislation meant very little—only seven people out of the 140 million eligible voted in the '94 Congressional elections. Upward mobility, the American way, provided a more lasting solution—the second-homeless have through extraordinary effort now joined the ranks of those who once rejected them.

Recent summers, however, give ominous evidence of another struggle in the offing. Those who have moved up to three or more homes report sightings of well-heeled derelicts in the exclusive enclaves of Nevis, Tuscany, County Cork, and elsewhere.

The third-homeless are upon us.

A HARDENING OF THE ARTS

ALTHOUGH New York City remained the hub of the international art and antiques world during the 1990s, the monopolization of art became less a matter of geography than of sheer wealth as the upward spiral of auction prices shrank the pool of potential buyers. Indeed, there are now only two important

collectors—publisher Si Newhouse and entertainer–turned–investment banker Bill Cosby. Newhouse (whose advertising-only cosmetics magazine for five-to-twelve-year-old girls, *Pink Celebrity,* launched in 1995, is already the most profitable Condé Nast publication) has been the sole bidder at several recent auctions. Cosby, chairman of Cosby, Kluge, Kohlberg, and Kravis, has had to lease the western Massachusetts towns of Stockbridge and Lenox as repositories for his collection of all extant Shaker furniture.

Still, Manhattan is where the action is. Although the short-lived, three-billion-dollar New York art futures market dissolved in the wake of the 1995 Wyethgate scandal (artist Andrew Wyeth "discovered" a vast new cache of Helga and Christian paintings hidden away at his Maine farm), and while major museums have had to cut back their acquisition activity (the Museum of Modern Art purchased its last new work, a sixteen-million-dollar Basquiat crayon-on-tablecloth, in 1996), the great arts

institutions are hardly dormant. Just last spring the Whitney Museum of American Art From the Early 1980s unveiled its "ninth and absolutely final" revised Michael Graves design, this one featuring an onyx and platinum facade, for its proposed expansion. And the new high-rise addition to the Guggenheim Museum proved uncontroversial when finally completed in 1995, perhaps because the original Frank Lloyd Wright museum building had been razed and replaced the previous year by the Metropolitan Museum of Art's new party Annex and SuperShop.

Not that art itself has gotten short shrift in the age of the nine-figure canvas. The Whitney's annual retrospective show of the work of David Salle and Julian Schnabel still draws literally dozens of art-hungry New Yorkers every year, and attendance at the Frick has actually *increased* since 1997, when it swapped its entire collection of Old Masters, eighteenth and nineteenth century works, for two especially fine Jasper Johns sketches.

The first antique nuclear weapon ever auctioned (at Christie's in 1997, for $122,000) was a mint 1949 vintage 2-kiloton atom bomb, nicknamed "Dumbo"

Faced with declining interest in their work among the general public, some artists have turned intramural. Typography artist Barbara Kruger, for instance, now devotes herself almost exclusively to assembling billboard-sized commentaries on the work of word painter Ed Ruscha. And the current Neo Neo Geo movement—that group of well-hyped young artists who appropriate and recycle, for ironic effect, the ironically recycled mid-80s images of the Neo Geo artists—is capturing the imagination of the intelligentsia from Soho to Tribeca.

For would-be patrons who lack the wherewithal to assemble a significant collection of original art, prices in the collectibles market have remained relatively low. A collection of *Ghostbuster IV* toys in good condition recently sold at Sotheby's for $13,000, less than half the presale estimate. It is at Christie's Contemporary Antiques sale this coming winter, however, that the most widely anticipated piece of the season is to go on the block: the auction house expects a U.S. government prototype hydrogen bomb (1953, steel and plutonium, E. Teller designer) to sell for at least $3.6 million.

HIZZONER! WILLIAM MURRAY, MAYOR OF CHICAGO

ACTUALLY you're lucky to catch me here today. I'm just about to join the rest of the city council in Kauai, where they're working on Chicago's urban congestion problems. (It's a lot easier to get some perspective on the situation from a distance.) Kauai is one of our sister cities. So is Tahiti. They spend their money here, then we take it and spend it over there.

We've been subsidizing the El Ruk'n to act as international antiterrorist swat teams. A lot of these kids have never been out of the country so they get a geography lesson while they're performing acts of community service. Since we're a hub city they can get to pretty much anywhere in the world. They meet people *and* they tell people about Chicago.

You initiated the project to pave over Lake Michigan to create more housing. Do you feel that this venture has been successful?

It's a catch-22 situation. There are people who want in there for any reason, at any cost, and yet they know there are some inherent dangers, but what do you do? How can you protect them? They're the Lewis and Clark of today. But by allowing them [the buildings] to be built there, we had to waive some of the usual building codes. We feel we opened things up for the pioneers of the nineties. Real estate that had been for many years claimed by some as one of the world's great lakes. If they're willing to risk the force of nature, God's speed and more power to them. I hope and pray that those buildings will stay standing for many years, long after I'm gone. The odds are, the first big storm's gonna rip them to shreds.

Is there any truth to the rumor that Ed Vrdolyac is buried beneath one of those buildings?

It would be wrong for me to comment on that at this time. Perhaps when the buildings have been knocked down. Let me say this, if anyone did do that it would have been very stupid to have buried him there. If he were.

Against all odds the Chicago Cubs won the '97 World Championship the first year you were in office. But a variety of charges have placed an asterisk against that victory. Would you care to explain?

It's a shame a great victory has to be tainted by charges of food poisoning.

But every restaurant the opposing team went to the same thing happened.

It was just a tragic set of freak circumstances.

Your first year in office was an amazing year for Chicago sports fans. The Cubs won, the Bears won, the Blackhawks won, and the Bulls finally won the basketball championship. All in the same year. Was that just a coincidence—were they inspired by your administration?

You'd have to attribute it to hard work, good coaching, teamwork, and, some would say, food poisoning.

Your daring plan of linking the two airports with one long runway met with a lot of controversy. Would you care to comment on that?

There are a lot of people upset about that. The 1.8 million people who had to be relocated.

But was it for the good of the city, or for the benefit of the airline you have shares in?

Well, you can't say that I have a favorite airline. I hold shares in all of them.

Do you feel you are sensitive to the many diverse factions within the city?

Certainly. When the people on Lakeshore Drive got upset with their real estate assessments, I knocked down a building and built them an outdoor public swimming pool.

It seems as if every Chicago administration has been riddled with corruption. Why do you think that is, and has yours been any different?

He's no clown with figures. Chicago Mayor Bill Murray balances the budget with money from his most recent fundraiser—John Wayne Gacy Day!

It's a tough town. You don't make it in this world without friends. Friendship is one of the things that built this city. And will continue to rebuild it. Over and over again.

Many officials have a building named in their honor, usually after they've left office. During your administration nearly every public landmark has had its name changed to yours: O'Murray Airport, the John Murray Building, Lake Murray . . .

Well, I think people need someone to thank. You wake up in the morning and you wanna thank somebody. And with so many different names on things, there's so much confusion; "Should I thank the Michigan, a tribe of Indians who no longer live in this area? How can you thank people who are no longer around? You really want somebody who's there. You want a guy you can get on the phone. A guy you can thank with a phone call, or a contribution.

It's true that you're the most loved politician that Chicago has ever known. Would you say that was because you gave everyone a dollar before the election or because of your public works?

Well, Chicago is known as the city that works. It always has been. And I try to make Chicago known as the city that works and plays. We play hard and we party hard.

What do you think your most lasting achievement has been so far?

I'll be known for morning fireworks. It goes with the feeling. It's like a get-up-and-go kind of feeling the city has. The idea of setting off fireworks in the morning is like driving a convertible with the top down and the air conditioner on. It's the ultimate sense of freedom. A belt-and-suspenders kind of feeling. It gets the propeller on your back spinning, you know? Takes you up off the ground and makes you fly. If we can set off fireworks in the daytime we can do anything.

Do you have any particular plans for your next term?

What I'd really like to do in the next three or four years is entrench myself for the next twenty years.

Do you have aspirations for higher office? Presidency?

I would but I couldn't afford the cut in pay.

With the shares from all the various airlines and the royalties you get from having your name on buildings here, I could see that you would have to take a substantial cut.

Just the idea of reporting gifts is alien to me. I think a gift is a personal thing. And why are gifts wrapped? Because it's personal. Nobody else's business. Why do you put a bow on it? So you can tell that it's personal. It's nobody's business.

And you have received a lot of gifts. In fact now that Sears has vacated to the Hoffman Estates, there's talk that it will become a storehouse for your gifts. Is that true?

Storehouse. I like to think of it as more of a viewing area. Storehouse to me says dusty. Of holding things up. I like to think of it as . . . you know, kind of like one of those log cabins kids used to have in their backyards? It's like that for me. A place where I can go to be alone with my gifts.

Every adminstration is accused of nepotism. Yours is no exception. Is it pure coincidence that everyone with the name of Murray is employed in some capacity by the city? Are they all qualified individuals?

I think it's crafty. The ones who are my relatives are working hard. As hard as they can work. The ones that aren't my relatives are inspiring. Leading by example. This particular person can make it just on a name. . . . People don't know if a person is or isn't related, you know. It's like "Is that gun loaded or not?" You're respected whether you know it or not.

After your election, charges were made that many of the people who voted for you were in fact dead.

"No strings attached," quipped Mayor Bill Murray, at the unveiling of
Philip Johnson's Tampon building in Chicago in 1996.

Well, I think of death not so much as the end of something, but more of a beginning, a transformation of one form of life to another. Or to a higher state. And I don't think that one should be punished from going from a lower state to a higher state. Certainly I don't think you should lose your right to vote. And if you read your Shirley MacLaine, all this is backed up.

Are you a follower of Miss MacLaine's beliefs?

I'm on some of the same mailing lists. Actually I've been in constant contact with Shirley ever since her death in 1991.

You often dispense with the three-piece business suit and go to work in a fireman's outfit, a janitorial uniform, etc. Today you're dressed as a clown. Does this indicate contempt for the office of mayor or as is it an attempt to identify with the common man?

I would like people to think that I'm just like they are. The only thing I could think of was to wear the same kind of clothes. The clown suit I'm wearing today, though, is to celebrate John Wayne Gacy day. I dress as John Gacy. I entertain for a while, have a big party for the kids, and then it sort of breaks up and gets crazy for a while. Then there's sort of a mock electrocution thing we do at the end of the day, and my nose lights up. Fun for everybody.

W here A re

Walt Disney

Thirty years after his death in 1966, Disney was removed from his cryonic-frost state, his fatal condition corrected and his life restored. He resumed his position as head of the vast Disney empire and remained there for two years, until April 1998, when he was shot and killed by Annette Funicello after trying to seduce the former Mouseketeer on the Disney Monorail at Disneyland in Anaheim, California. His body was refrozen and awaits corrective procedures pending a lawsuit barring them filed by Funicello.

Christine Keeler

Ten years ago she set the dubious record of appearing on 645 TV talk and interview shows in forty eight hours, promoting either a book or a movie—no one can remember which. She returned to her native England where she manufactured and sold copies of a molded plywood chair inspired by a design by Charles Eames.

The Exxon Valdez

The infamous oil tanker that in 1989 was responsible for the largest oil spill in U.S. history. The tanker cruised the world for ten years, and was denied admission to every port until August of this year when it won the

America's Cup and was welcomed back to its original berth in Wilmington, Delaware.

The Los Angeles Dodgers

In 1996 the team was bought by Malcolm Forbes who returned the Dodgers to Brooklyn. Forbes built an inflatable replica of Ebbets Field and forced the team to play baseball 5,000 feet in the air. When no opponents were forthcoming Forbes dumped the Dodgers into Sheepshead Bay where they eventually became a succession of nine-man synchronized swimming teams.

Brandon Tartikoff

The "wunderkind" programming chief of NBC, who led his network from last place to first during his tenure, was dismissed when he was discovered molesting a Smurf. He returned to his original job as a Wednesday luncheon special at the Russian Tea Room.

David Seville

The creator of the Chipmunks was accused by the Animal Rescue League of using the small animals in medical experiments. The case reached the Supreme Court, which decided to let the individual states determine how to deal with such matters.

Shields & Yarnell

The mime team, who enjoyed a modest success in the 70s and 80s, retired in 1993 and married Tai Babilonia and Randy Gardner, the

unlucky skating hopefuls of the 1976 Olympics. The four currently pose for jungle gym designers at an Indiana playground equipment factory.

Alan Thicke

Eighties TV personality who is best remembered for winning a lookalike contest because he looked like both Shields *and* Yarnell. Thicke felt his career had peaked with that victory, whereupon he retired from public life after a grateful public offered him thirty million dollars to do so.

Yoko Ono

The widow of John Lennon. At the time of his death the couple owned several apartments in the Dakota, a luxury co-op apartment building in New York. Yoko continued to buy more apartments in the building until she eventually owned all of them. In 1996 she was convicted of murdering all the Dakota co-op owners, including Lauren Bacall, Warner LeRoy, Rex Reed, and Leonard Bernstein, for the purpose of buying their apartments. She is currently serving a life sentence at the Dannemora State Prison for Women, where she has already bought 95 percent of the prison cells.

Baby Harp Seals

The cute little things which were the darlings of animal rights organizations and environmental protection groups were organized into a nation by Brigitte Bardot who bought them an island in the North Sea. Bardot was elected their president in a free election, and in 1998 they were invaded by a nation of fur-novelty manufacturers. Bardot escaped the invading forces, but vows to return even if her country is only a couple of million key-chain ornaments.

The Broadway Theater

By the opening of the '91 theater season, an orchestra seat to a Broadway hit cost $1,199.95. Genuine lovers of theater found an alternative, however, in the increasingly sophisticated shows presented by performers in subway stations. Most of these still cost whatever one cared to contribute, although some groups, particularly those presenting entire plays or symphonies, were beginning to charge a dollar a head upfront. Soon crowds waiting for *Godot* equaled those waiting to return to Queens. Ends of platforms were cordoned off, lights and seats installed, and "Under-Broadway Theater" was born. Under-Off-Broadway and Under-Off-Off-Broadway soon followed. By mid-decade most Manhattan subway stations offered full-scale productions. Prices ranged from a high of about $24.95 for a seat on exit ramps, to $1.98 for the third rail. Only one aboveground theater survived, Gregory Mosher's Lincoln City Hall—an amalgam of Lincoln Center, City Center, and Radio City Music Hall. In 1996 it was converted into a subway station. Current price for a front-row exit ramp seat at a Lloyd Webber Under-Broadway musical is $899.95 and rising.

The "Rightist" Brothers
—Norman Podhoretz and Pat Buchanan

It was in 1992 that Norman Podhoretz penned his most passionate exegesis of why the West must be defended even when it is not threatened, and first coined the term "Judeo-Saxon ethic." Unfortunately for Podhoretz no one either noticed or was offended. There were fewer more pathetic victims of the Cold Peace than right-wingers who had fought the Cold War from the foxholes of their PCs. Deprived of a raison d'être, they became desperate. In the spring of '92, the "Rightist Brothers," Podhoretz and Buchanan, hatched a plan (code name "Commie Posses R Us") to start World War III themselves. Other soon-to-be-unemployed hard-liners—Emmett Tyrrel, Jr., Elliot Abrams, Chris Buckley, among others —joined up. The group targeted a remote missile silo in Wyoming. Claiming it revolted him but that anything was permissible to avoid the "nightmare of peace," Buchanan acquired the access, arming, and firing codes by seducing a young Air Force lieutenant and then blackmailing him.

The assault on the silo was well-planned and well-executed, and involved shooting all the surface guards. (This precipitated the only hitch: Elliot Abrams was so terrified by the sound of actual gunfire that he soiled himself and had to return to the motel.) The group made it to the command center, and then armed and targeted the missile, but at that point, according to survivors, the silo cap malfunctioned, refusing to open. Podhoretz and Buchanan volunteered to open it manually and both were actually sitting on the warhead when the missile launched without warning. Happily it went nowhere near its target, exploding several minutes later at the wrong point in its trajectory, and the Rightist Brothers were, in every sense, history.

Arnold Schwarzenegger

Maria Shriver's husband was an unfortunate victim of the Kennedy Family Plan. The plan, formulated in 1996 at a family convention in Hyannisport, was to "create" one million Kennedys by the year 2050. The family was vague about how this was to be achieved but the Kennedy women were not. Schwarzenegger was constantly in demand and his sense of duty to his new family prompted him to oblige. He dropped 100 pounds, became addicted to steroids, and was eventually admitted to a private mental home after attempting to castrate himself. He is currently listed as "beyond therapy."

 A r e W  h e r e ?

"If Lenny were alive today, he'd be behind everything I do," avowed Andrew Dice Clay, seconds before his penis was shot off on the night of August 7, 1991. Clay—described by Tom Shales as "America's most telling and incisive satirist of human foibles"—climaxed his routine by inviting either a black or a woman to come up to the stage and then urinating on them. The young black woman who volunteered on the night of August 7th happened to be an off-duty police officer. Her retaliatory act was condemned instantly by the comic community as an "outrageous infringement of the Dicer's freedom of speech." The Patrolman's Benevolent Association named her Markswoman of the Year.

America's 7.4 Million Stand-Up Comedians

Reliable estimates put the number of stand-up comedians in the United States as of Labor Day 1991 at 7.4 million. Roughly one-third of this number had made a twenty-second appearance on one of the nation's seventy five round-the-clock comedy channels. The rest swelled the ranks of the "humorless"—destitute comedians who camped around comedy clubs, TV studios, and concert halls, looking for fresh material or a free tryout. Many communities passed laws against the humorless, in particular their practice of asking local citizens, "Where are you from?" and then insulting them.

Judy Tenuta, president of the National Coalition for the Humorless, pleaded with the White House to establish emergency "stand-up

shelters" for the humorless, or failing that a Special Special Task Force to acquire several inexpensive cable channels to ensure the humorless their "constitutional right to a half-hour special."

Whoever was president at the time failed to respond, so the comic community set about taking care of its own. Friars Club president Billy Crystal organized a charity show called "Comics on Relief" during the summer of '93. It was a disaster. Seven hundred thousand comedians "volunteered" to make an appearance at the two-hour event; the only people who showed up at the Hollywood Bowl were the humorless themselves. Sam Kinison, who opened the show, was trampled to death when the audience rushed the stage en masse to get hold of his mike.

The ensuing riot prompted California to make stand-up comedy illegal as of January 1, 1994. Most states followed suit; some even outlawed public discussion of airline travel, Asian driving habits, and late-night local television commercials.

THE MIRACLE OF DEMOCRACY

THE MIRACLE OF DEMOCRACY it was not. At one point in the mad mid-90s, there were four Presidents, the Cabinet had more members than Congress, and the World Court had just garnished the Federal budget. Miraculously the people (demos) reasserted their rule (cracy), and democracy triumphed. In short the system works. As a very wise man once said: If it ain't broke, don't fix it.

THE MIRACLE OF DEMOCRACY

*"It was my first public appearance in ten years where no one took
a swing at me" was how President-elect Geraldo Rivera
remembered his swearing in ceremony.*

BEHIND THE BUSHES

GEORGE Michael Thomas Bush spent the last year of his term in hiding. The official reason was that he was "giving further study" to the question of whether the official state bird of the District of Columbia should be the yellow tit. The real reason was that he was avoiding Mikhail Gorbachev.

The importunate chairman of the Russian Not-So-Communist Party had by now unilaterally demobilized his entire air, sea, and land forces, scrapped his nuclear arsenal, and converted all his conventional weaponry to such civilian use as mobile Laundromats. He actually took up residence in Washington, D.C. for several months in the spring of '92, "to be available for meetings" with the elusive chief executive. For his part, Bush began to suffer what one medical adviser described as an acute "military-industrial complex." At one point, according to insiders, he contemplated asking the Joint Chiefs to stage a military coup and proclaim the United States "the greatest banana republic in history" and himself leader in perpetuity of the Banana Republican Party. True or not, he issued standing orders in May '92 that no one in the White House was to answer the door or the phone.

Few Americans cared what Bush did; his thin credibility had disappeared. Democratic revelations that members of Reagan's cabinet —Bush included—had routinely stolen spare change from one another's jackets in the White House cloakroom completed the work done by earlier HUD and Pentagon scandals. Bush's countermoves were increasingly transparent. In

his 1990 State of the Union address he declared that the answer to America's social woes was "eight hundred points of light." By the 1991 State of the Union address these had become—mysteriously—"six hundred and forty points of light." Surgery to alter his voice from a goatlike tenor to an impressive basso profundo was unsuccessful. His proposal to change the Second Amendment to read "the right to bear surplus arms" did nothing to assuage his restless right wing, and was vetoed by Congress. His wife's elaborate attempt to launch a "uniside" fashion for mature women ("You can't tell the back from the front!") was a tremendous flop.

But it was in the financial arena that Bush's embarrassments were greatest. Typically the Bush approach to an economic crisis was not to address it, but to distract attention from it. Campaigning for reelection in '92, for instance, Bush insisted that America's massive trade imbalance was no problem. The number of America's exports would soar during his second term, he said, because he was declaring 1995 the International Year of the Discount.

The most notorious Bush administration economic gimmick, however, was the widely touted Deficit-Aid concert held in New Or-

WHAT NORIEGA HAD ON BUSH

The Panamanian strongman's mysterious ability to defy President Bush was finally explained when shortly before his death, Noriega released this candid shot of their 1985 meeting.

leans on July 4, 1992. Organized by Republican party chairman Lee "Muddy" Atwater, the huge event was designed to bring together the greatest names in R & B, and through a global hookup raise billions to offset the national debt (by then running at 310 billion dollars a year or almost exactly the same as the defense budget). Atwater, who had just released a highly successful album, *Sold, Man!*, which included his own R & B classics "Nobody Knows the Truffles I've Seen" and "Got My Modem Workin'," was in a jocular mood on the big night.

He addressed the assembled artists, who included such legendary names as B.B. King, Rufus and Carla Thomas, Sam Moore, Albert Collins, and many others. "It's you boys what caused this here deficit mess," said Atwater, vamping on his guitar, "Ashley," "what with your whorin' and fightin' and dopin' and such. Least you can do now is help out some. A-one, a-two, a-one, two, three—"

They were his last words. And to all intents and purposes they were the last words of the Bush administration.

How the Right Made the Center Fold

PRESIDENTIALLY speaking, the mid-nineties was a time of chaos, when a person's political affiliation could be guessed not so much by whom they'd picked for president as who they *thought* was president.

Officially, the Quayle-Quayle ticket won the '92 election in a landslide. But the results were mitigated by an acceleration of the decline in voter turnouts of the 80s. Only 7 percent of eligible voters cast ballots in '92; the over-whelming majority of these voted for Michael J. Fox.

Fox's hugely successful series "This Old White House," in which he played a youthful and irreverent president, complicated the political process in unforeseen ways. A poll taken by the *New York Times* in 1993 revealed that 63 percent of Americans thought Fox was president. Of the remainder, 28 percent thought he was doing a better job than whoever was president.

The confusion was compounded by imitators (at one point in the '94 TV season, there were seventeen series on the air set in the White House), and by media interdiction on the part of various political groups. One animal rights group, for example, regularly broke into scheduled cable and network broadcasts with news stories about "President Max" (an appealing four-year-old Labrador) and a compliant Congress of liberated lab animals. Media security forces were powerless to prevent these intrusions: viewers not only accepted the veracity of the bulletins, but approved of the legislative harmony between President Max and the Congress of Rats.

Even more popular was "President Judy." According to this version of events in Washington, Republican president Judy had beaten the Democratic presidential candidate—also called Judy—in '92, and was now trouncing a recalcitrant male Congress with one political triumph after another.

Although President Judy was believed at the time to be the fabrication of the underground Women's Media Caucus, it is possible that for a season she may actually have been president. The only existing record of the pe-

Marilyn Quayle's startling attempt at self-promotion did little for her husband's 1992 campaign.

riod is on videotape, and there are strong indications that a woman *was* president from 1994–96. Some telehistorians claim that this was President Marilyn Quayle, who was elected vice president in '92 and assumed the presidency after her husband's mysterious "ascension into heaven" during a Christmas skiing vacation in 1993. This explanation portrays President Marilyn as so deranged that her advisers encouraged the confusion with President Judy in order to stay in power, even inviting President Judy to live in the White House with President Marilyn. They further argue that while Judy was not chosen by the old pre-media method of balloting, because she was the most popular of the dozens of presidents on the air at the time, she was a Constitutionally tele-elected chief executive.

On the legislative side, Congress was an equally shadowy presence. One (written) document from May 1993 indicates that 70 percent of the Senate members were absent from Washington on that date, primarily because they were on speaking tours, writing books, or completing committee reports in the Caribbean with research teams of Senate pages. In the House, meanwhile, legislation was proposed making House seats hereditary.

Any corroboration by the ancient method of news footage is at this point next to impossible. The mid-nineties saw the last gasp of network news, as reportage gave way to surer methods of attracting viewers. Even if network news heads had any interest in covering so deadly a subject as Washington politics, it's unlikely viewers would have given much credence to programs that were more often topless than topical. News programs that had measurable ratings during the period included NBC's "Hideous Grisly Tasteful Network Murders" with Tom Brokaw, CBS's "Watch Them Die" with Connie Chung, and "Dead Nude Models Live at Five" on CNN (Cable Nudes Network).

THE SITCOM CONGRESS

ON November 8, 1996, show business finally achieved the preeminent position in American life for which it had been preparing itself for almost a hundred years. Celebrity, the mark of the aristocrat in a society without an aristocracy, finally became the standard by which we consented to be ruled.

Said President Rivera in his inaugural message: "Are not those we elect with our love and admiration better suited in every way to run this country than those we are compelled to choose from a corrupt and outdated party system.

Yes, yes, and yes again. The election of '96, the first in which votes were registered by viewers directly on their video screens, was a triumph for a power structure whose beauty and talent had been the unacknowledged fulcrum of American political and social life. Both houses of Congress were swept clean of politicians and filled with stars. The Supreme Court was tele-impeached and restocked with men and women who had demonstrated their compassion and sense of fair play innumerable times out in the open—instead of behind closed doors in dusty chambers. Cabinet officers were appointed not by presidential whim but by an informed public. It took two wild, sometimes wacky, but always entertaining hours, and when the new Congress, cabinet, and court assembled at the end of the show to sing its theme song "My Way" en masse, the nation had a government like none other

The "Sitcom" Supreme Court: Left to right (Top row): Justice Malden, Justice Wapner, Justice Winfrey, Justice Mister Rogers. (Bottom row): Justice Marshall (dec.), Justice Falk, Chief Justice Bennie, Justice Shatner, Justice Keith.

before it, an admired and trusted government.

The new Congress became known affectionately as the "Sitcom Congress"—a misnomer, really, since many of its members had appeared in dramatic series—and its achievements have kept pace with those first heady expectations. Recognizing that what the electorate wants is a continuum of reassuring faces and messages, interspersed with occasional decisive victories over internal or external enemies, it appointed its best-known and best-loved colleagues to key chairmanships, and never passes legislation—or chose an enemy—without exhaus-

tive polling. The days when America could be randomly put under siege by some foreign maniac are gone forever. Now *we* take the initiative, *we* pick our foes, and, whether we actually fight them or not, *we* win.

Giving people exactly what they want has been criticized by a few as a dereliction of leadership. Neither the many, nor its leaders, agree. "Leadership is a fascist concept," said New Age Immortal and former Secretary of Tummies, Fannies, and Breast-Feeding, Jane Fonda, shortly before her death. "In a free society you can only lead by following."

Where the Power is: Key Committees

AGRICULTURE, NUTRITION, AND FORESTRY (Senate)
Eddie Albert (Oliver Wendell Douglas, "Green Acres")
Michael Landon (Charles Ingalls, "Little House on the Prairie")
Laurence Tureaud (Mr. T, "The A-Team")

ARMED SERVICES (Senate)
Jim Nabors (Gomer Pyle, "Gomer Pyle, U.S.M.C.")
Alan Alda (Capt. Hawkeye Pierce, "M*A*S*H")
Ernest Borgnine (Lt. Cdr. Quinton McHale, "McHale's Navy")
Robert Conrad (Maj. Gregory "Pappy" Boyington, "Baa Baa Black Sheep")

BUDGET (Senate)
Pat Sajak, Monty Hall, Bob Barker, Gene Rayburn, Chuck Woolery

DISTRICT OF COLUMBIA (House)
Jimmie Walker (J.J. Evans, "Good Times")
Clifton Davis (Clifton Curtis, "That's My Mama")
Ted Lange (Junior, "That's My Mama")
Cleavon Little (Dr. Jerry Noland, "Temperatures Rising")
Malcolm Jamal Warner (Theodore Huxtable, "The Cosby Show")

EDUCATION AND LABOR (House)
Education:
Robin Givens (Darlene, "Head of the Class")
Gabe Kaplan (Gabe Kotter, "Welcome Back, Kotter")
Labor:
Carroll O'Connor (Archie Bunker, "All in the Family")
Ed Asner ("Lou Grant")

ENERGY AND NATURAL RESOURCES (Senate)
Larry Hagman (J.R. Ewing, "Dallas")
John Forsythe (Blake Carrington, "Dynasty")

FOREIGN RELATIONS (Senate)
Ricardo Montalban (Mr. Roarke, "Fantasy Island")
Herve Villechaize (Tattoo, "Fantasy Island")
John Hillerman (Jonathan Quale Higgins III, "Magnum, P.I.")

HOUSE ADMINISTRATION
Ted Cassidy (Lurch, "The Addams Family")
Robert Guillaume ("Benson")
Christopher Hewett (Mr. Lyn Belvedere, "Mr. Belvedere")

INTERIOR AND INSULAR AFFAIRS (House)
Dan Haggerty (James "Grizzly" Adams, "The Life and Times of Grizzly Adams")
Bob Denver (Gilligan, "Gilligan's Island")

How a Bill Becomes a Law

1 An outline for a bill is submitted to a given senator or congressman by the appropriate agency (e.g., GCM—Global Creative Management—or the CIAA). *2* The senator / congressman requests funding for a "treatment" of the proposed bill. The treatment includes up to a dozen potential different "story lines" or scenarios of how the bill would work in practice. *3* The appropriate chairpersons "do leg" (legislation) over an informal meal, to discuss which of the scenarios will "play" to the House and Senate. *4* They agree on a step-deal. The bill is now a "go." *5* The chosen scenario is written into a brief film, comedic or dramatic depending on the nature of the bill (e.g., pollution would be played comedically, terminal disease dramatically). It usually stars its sponsoring senator or congressman. *6* The film version of the bill is screened for the House and the Senate. Each member votes "yes" or "no" with an audience survey device attached to his or her seat. If a majority of both houses "loves" the bill, it is pronounced a "hit." *7* The bill is now law.

POST OFFICE AND CIVIL SERVICE (House)
John Ratzenberger (Cliff Clavin, "Cheers")
S. Epatha Merkerson (Reba, "Pee-Wee's Playhouse")

SCIENCE, SPACE, AND TECHNOLOGY (House)
Robin Williams (Mork, "Mork and Mindy")
Larry Hagman (Capt. Anthony Nelson, "I Dream of Jeannie")

Sally Field (Sister Bertrille, "The Flying Nun")
Bill Bixby (David Bruce Banner, "The Incredible Hulk")
Lee Majors (Steve Austin, "The Six Million Dollar Man")

SELECT AGING (House)
Gary Coleman (Arnold Jackson, "Diff'rent Strokes")

SELECT INTELLIGENCE (Senate)
Peter Graves (James Phelps, "Mis-

sion: Impossible")

SELECT NARCOTICS ABUSE AND CONTROL (House)
Don Johnson (Det. Sonny Crockett, "Miami Vice")
Robert Blake (Tony Baretta, "Baretta")
Kristy McNichol (Letitia "Buddy" Lawrence, "Family")

WAYS AND MEANS (House)
Henry Winkler (Arthur Fonzarelli, "Happy Days")

1 Women shall not be presented in a negative light in any medium. 2 If women must be portrayed in a less than positive light due to historical circumstance (e.g., the life story of Eva Braun), they shall be portrayed as unwitting victims of a male-dominated system. 3 In such isolated cases where women in public life (or characters representing them in the media) have committed objectively illegal, unethical, or immoral acts, they shall always be portrayed as the unwitting victims of a male-dominated system. 4 All success and/or preeminence achieved by women in any field of endeavor shall be presented equally and uncritically, however questionable the legal, ethical, or moral standards of the field of endeavor, or the means by which the success was achieved. 5 Aggression in personal relationships, contempt for natural life forms, exploitation of the underclass, victimization of the poor, old, or young, espousal of crypto-military corporate concepts such as "winning," "taking no prisoners," etc., shall be presented as obnoxious if pursued by a male, and courageous, pioneering, and beneficial to the women's movement if pursued by a woman. 6 No woman involved in education, educational theory, educational media, or any other activity pertaining to the upbringing of children shall be required to have children of her own. 7 The right of women to use their bodies, and/or other women's bodies, to sell clothing, cosmetics, cars, food, beverages, drugs, real estate, financial services, travel and transportation, leisure products, or any other goods, through the use of titillation, arousal, incitement to sexual congress or any other legitimate sales technique, shall be inviolable. 8 Rape shall always be presented as the ultimate crime. 9 The use of terms and concepts such as "sexism," "phallocracy," etc., shall be presented as naive when applied to political issues (e.g., defense, racism), but apposite and compelling in discussions of income differential and sexual harassment. 10 All accounts of the recent history of the women's movement shall portray its early commitment to fight exploitation, poverty, environmental destruction, and militarism as naive and/or youthful exuberance. The development of priorities such as income and personal health and enhancement may be presented humorously, but not sarcastically. The use of irony, or saying something other than what is meant to dramatize its absurdity, is absolutely prohibited.

EVERYBODY WORKS!

FROM the diary of Carter van Penciltier, Secretary of Human Resources.

February 5, 1995

I have been invited by my friend the president to join her cabinet, and have been handed a herculean mandate: to bring this country to 100 percent employment within two years.

April 15

Return from vacation brings first major crisis. The concept of full employment sounds great. But now it dawns on me—just where the heck are these jobs going to come from? I'm asking everyone: mostly I get a lot of shrugs. It's on the tip of my tongue to ask the wonderful Filipino woman who does for us around the house.

June 15

I am marshaling experts. My economics advisor is one Harrison Gray Janeway—the fellow who does "Consumer Probe" on Channel Q446. Surprised to learn he hadn't gone to Harvard. I mean the guy is smart as all get-out. Well, over a few drinks last night at Trader Vic's (Tiki Pukka-Pukkas, as I recall) he sketched out *one whale* of a theory on a cocktail napkin. He calls it "Trickle-Up" and it sounds smart. Darn smart. I jammed the napkin in my pocket and raced into the Oval Office first thing this afternoon and well, my good pal the president says she's going to just *ram* it through Congress—as only she can.

Trickle-Up works like this: the fed provides tax incentives for various Americans in the top earning brackets. Rich people for instance. This in turn makes it easier for them to hire more household staff, hence providing more jobs.

September 4

We are beginning to see the return of the footman, the gamekeeper, the scullery maid. The word around town is: "It's so easy to find good help these days!" Employment levels are creeping upward. 90 percent, 91 percent, 91.5 percent.

December 24

The president has hired a jester. A wonderful funny fellow. A Jew. Because of my own busy schedule I have found a woman to sit on the edge of my armchair in the rumpus room and

Nature calls, and the roving Bathroom Brigade responds.
Tip them well—they have a hard time getting into restaurants on their lunch break.

watch TV for me while I read. From time to time she taps me on the shoulder and says: "I think this might interest you, sir." And this woman was on welfare for eleven years! 94 percent and climbing!

January 6, 1996
Trickle-Up is working well, but we need new gimmicks. I woke up this morning with this echoing in my head: "Any job worth doing is more worth doing for two or more people." Catchy. *Teamwork* will be the word of the year. Driver and co-drivers on buses. Every subway car will have a conductor. A coin-and-bottle team on every Coke machine. Busboys will have assistant busboys. Twenty-four-hour Human ATMs can have *two* humans!

March 15
"Punch and Judy Banking" they're calling it. But I don't mind. In fact, I tried to track down the person who thought that phrase up, so I could make it his job to have thought it up. 95.5 percent!

June 22
I panicked today. It suddenly dawned on me that many, many *children* are unemployed. I got on the horn to see about reopening dormant coal mines. Bingo! 96 percent!

June 30

This whole Punch and Judy thing is going wild! Companies are adopting "relay race" systems. For instance bike messenger routes are being broken up into smaller and smaller segments so that everyone gets a chance to carry the package part of the way! The post office plans to introduce Your Personal Postman—a carrier for every address. Seven fire departments I know of have started bucket brigades. Oh, they lost a few buildings, sure. But those buildings have to be rebuilt—and painted and furnished and landscaped and . . . you got it! 97 percent and counting!

July 4. Independence Day

We've found the North Slope of Alaska of employment! Teams of smartly uniformed urinal operators. It does my heart good to see their smiling faces and jaunty little caps as they wait proudly in their neat rows to flush for me. Other men and women go around with big manila envelopes and long tweezers and leave pubic hairs on the edges of toilets. Still others are being employed to remove the hairs. Call it busywork if you want, but it's jobs, darn it!

July 30

I think I may be what they're calling me—a genius. HIRE PEOPLE AS FURNITURE! A scantily clad young lady makes a lovely lamp. Sturdy former steelworkers gang up and boom! —a spacious, stylish sofa. 98.2 percent . . . 98.4 percent . . . 98.6 percent . . .

September 17

My very good friend the president called me in today. An unexpected side benefit: so many people are scrubbing, waxing, digging, pulling, carrying, or just plain sitting in the corner with a lampshade on, that hardly a single foreign-made, vital-juice-sapping dishwasher, automobile, or dining-room set was imported into America in the last quarter. Not only are we 98.7 percent employed, we're SELF-SUFFICIENT as well!

October 15

We have hit the wall at 99 percent employment and are stuck there like a sparrow in the grille of a Buick. Splat. Goosh. Can*not* budge those figures.

Trouble is—the election's only three weeks away. A few wags have started sporting buttons reading "Mr. 100%???" which really chafes my shorts. I have to think, think fast and hard.

October 16

GOT IT! A colossal "Work Makes You Free" rally in Bush Memorial Plaza. The huge red flags with the bold "%" signs snap in the wind. I stand in front of hundreds of thousands of my employed fellow countrymen (let off work for the day!). I tell them that what's holding us back from the magic 100 percent isn't lack of jobs, but a SURPLUS OF PEOPLE! People so unemployable they SAP the STRENGTH of our SUPER, SUPER nation like horrible parasitic LEECHES!

Editor's note:

This was the last entry in Mr. van Penciltier's diary. On November 3, 1996, he was shot dead by an assassin, former steelworker Joseph Testicola. Mr. Testicola was unemployed. In a tribute to the van Penciltier spirit, the president hired him on the spot, as White House Consultant on Assassinations.

99.00001 percent . . . WAY TO GO!

There's a place for everyone who wants to work. Right here in the living room. A little to the left. Right there. Perfect!

After the
successful
Poland LBO,
there was a
rush of countries
to go private.
Helmut Kohl
teamed with
Kohlberg Kravis
to do a leveraged
buyout of
West Germany.

MERGER MOST FOUL

FAR from disappearing from the scene, takeovers and leveraged buyouts became ever more innovative and gargantuan during the 1990s.

The disillusionment with corporate LBOs early in the decade soon dissipated as the trend went multi-international; but not before a series of junk bond conflagrations swept the U.S. in the summer of 1992, beginning with the celebrated "Bonfire of the Hamptons." Mobs of angry investors from Newport Beach to Palm Beach, chanting "Drexel burned me," ignited tens of billions of dollars in junk bonds that had become worthless when the companies issuing them sank into oblivion in the agonizing "quicksand recession" of 1992–93. However, efforts by Wall Street to pass a constitutional amendment prohibiting the burning of junk bonds went nowhere.

The nail-biting battle for Poland commenced in 1994 when Gen. Woijciech Jaruzelski, backed by the Bass brothers of Texas, made the opening move. They tried to buy the country upfront. Solidarity brought in Pope John Paul as a white knight. The Pope won out by resorting to a brilliant new financing technique devised by investment bankers Walesa, Wasserstein and Perella. With the value of art soaring to undreamed-of heights, Walessarella underwrote a $300 billion offering of "Cross my heart" bonds, collateralized by the Vatican collections. The voracious Disney Company gobbled up the offering of what were nicknamed monk bonds, and wound up with the Sistine Chapel and other works when the Pope missed two payments in 1997. Disney made a further killing when it auctioned off the Sistine Chapel by the square foot for $30 billion, in line with the trend to split important art into so-called "master pieces" because no one could afford entire works any longer. However, chips of the *Pieta* did not bring as much as Disney expected.

After the successful Poland LBO, there was a rush of countries to go private. Helmut Kohl teamed with Kohlberg Kravis to do a leveraged buyout of West Germany. KKK, as it was known, then did a takeover of East Germany, uniting the two parts for the first time since 1945. Colombia was bought in by the Medellin cartel. And Saul Steinberg and the Metropolitan Museum of Art combined to do a takeover of France, using the museum's art collection to back its offer. After selling off pieces of the *Mona Lisa* and *Winged Victory* to pay down debt, Steinberg moved the Louvre Museum to New York where it became the Gayfryd Louvre Steinberg wing of the Met.

The Soviet Union was forced to start divesting itself of some republics to come up with hard currency needed to implement *perestroika.* This was also the case for some Eastern European countries which shed provinces. This led to the creation of new "multi-internationals" such as Time-Warner-Estonia, Saab-Scania-Azerbaijan, and Hoechst-Hardy's-Herzegovina.

The offering of stock in individuals really took off in the mid-90s when England's Prince Charles, having fled England, went public to raise the money needed to snatch back the monarchy from Margaret Thatcher. Investors around the world eagerly snapped up the hot flotation. Prince Charles PLC leveraged the five billion pounds sterling raised in the offering to go on a global raiding spree, buying everything from Don King and Royal Dutch Petroleum to Prince Edward Island and King World Productions. Jimmy Goldsmith pro-

Masterpieces were so valuable that they became corporations and were often split up in takeovers and mergers. This is the top left-hand corner of Van Gogh's "Potato-Eaters" Inc., valued at 266 million dollars.

ceeded to buy Prince Charles in the largest individual takeover to that point. But Goldsmith was unable to fend off a bid for himself from Paul McCartney Etc.

The ultimate deal of the decade was the LBO of Japan in 1998. Japan triggered its own buyout when it made a bid for the parts of California, Washington, and Oregon (or the East Coast, as it is known in Tokyo), which it did not already own. But in a brilliant counterstroke, Disney organized "Pacific Overtures," a multitrillion dollar leveraged buyout fund which nabbed Nippon instead. Backers included Prudential-Purina-Bache Corp., IBM-Yves St. Laurent, Merrill Lynch/Meryl Streep Inc., S. G. Walmart Murdoch Reuters Bertelsmann Gannett Hachette Dow Jones Maxwell Newhouse Times Post and Tribune News World and Banque de Suez Sondheim Lloyd Webber.

**1996 was the
Year of the
Smell, when the
market became
fixated on
consumer stocks
involving odors.**

HERD ON THE STREET

THE stock market began its assault on the 4,000 level in April 1995. On the Big Board, Nintendo clocked the biggest move after introducing *Ninja Roach Motel,* an interactive video game that doubled as an insecticide. *U.S.A. Today's* 1995 introduction of the *rereadable newspaper*—"Stays Current for Weeks at a Time"—had a huge impact on media stocks, as did the *Atlantic's* decision to become the *Pacific.*

Disposable TVs from Korea and Taiwan devastated U.S. home electronics firms, but American industry fought back with such items as prenatal cellular phones and *blue-Collar New Age clothing*—digitally operated designer duds enabling factory workers to switch from dowdy workclothes to West Coast fashions by pressing a toggle switch. *Fanny Fondlers,* computer-programmed self-caressing foundation garments for the sex-starved, would have been the biggest consumer durable of the decade save for three electronic sodomies resulting from soft-ware glitches.

1996 was the Year of the Smell, when the market became fixated on consumer stocks involving odors. Procter & Gamble saw its stock double after introducing *Déjà Pew,* a retroactive sensory recall unit capable of retrieving pleasant smells that had left a room as long ago as twenty-four hours earlier.

The aging figured prominently in the hottest health stocks of the 1990s. The leader was Pangalactic Geriatric, a chain of mall-sized nursing homes orbiting the planet. PG zipped from its IPO price of $8 a share to $137 before federal regulators fined the firm 250 million dollars for operating racially segregated intergalactic nursing homes.

Elsewhere, Ominous Orthodontic was the first publicly traded company to capitalize on the *personal radon* scare, astutely determining that aging residents of Pennsylvania and New York who did not open their mouths often enough for them to become properly ventilated were getting radon trapped in their dentures. The first company to establish a dental radon test by mail, Ominous Orthodontic shot from $13 to $65.

Among food stocks, General Mills fared best with its *Gourmet Reptile* line, designed to appeal to those concerned with animals' rights. Far and away its most successful item were frozen frog's arms, tadpole breasts, reheatable loin of newt, and *Crapaud Stretcher.*

The animal interpretation business took off in 1995 after Pakistani scientists succeeded in cracking the secret language of camels. Companies specializing in translating the sounds and gestures of household pets into English traded at huge multiples on NASDAQ, and saw their stocks shoot into the stratosphere when federal prosecutors began using the testimony of brokerage house parakeets and goldfish to put crooked money managers behind bars. Top performers included *Cat Scanners* and the first emergency animal interpretation outfit: *Overnight Woofer.*

Perhaps the most notorious highflier of the 1990s was *Mr. Wraith.* In 1994, fraternity brothers at Michigan State inadvertently discovered that when hot water was funneled through a Melitta filter containing the cremated remains of the recently deceased, the dead returned to life. *Mr. Wraith,* modestly priced at $39.95, including Pyrex urn, became the hot Christmas item of 1995, with the legendary Jerry Della Femina slogan: "This Christmas Throw Momma Back on the Train."

Animal Rights groups changed America's eating habits. Uncuddly cold-blooded reptiles replaced cute furry mammals on American tables.

**May 1994:
Congress makes
even deeper cuts
in the U.S.
military budget.
The president
signs the bill,
but uses
someone else's
signature.**

SITTING ON DEFENSE

MIKHAIL Gorbachev's first act as elected Prime Minister of Most of the Russias was to withdraw eighty-five percent of the Soviet troops from Eastern Europe, leaving in place only janitorial specialists and PR officers. Further deep cuts in overall troop strength followed and soon career army officers were lining up outside the Moscow personnel offices of McDonald's and Kentucky Fried Chicken.

Public opinion in the United States demanded a serious response to the "Red Peace Menace." Early in 1992, the House passed a "revised" military budget, with 52 Republicans joining all 319 Democrats. The bill sailed through the Senate, making it all but veto-proof as it headed for the right-wing White House.

Congress and the White House slugged it out; however, the pace of events quickened:

*After budget cutbacks, the Pentagon became the Rectagon, and the
White House–Kremlin hotline switched to Sprint.*

March 1993: The U.S. withdraws from NATO, calling it "a million-dollar debating society." England, France, and West Germany follow suit. West Germany names its scaled-down army the "Greenbeans."

November 1993: Following the death of its last remaining octogenarian, China's politburo declares the "Thousand Neonizations" to take China into the twentieth century "before it is over."

April 1994: The Soviets and the Chinese announce a total shutdown of military production in favor of consumer goods. To attract foreign exchange, the Soviet's largest tank factory retools to turn out 1971 Ford Pintos.

May 1994: Congress makes even deeper cuts in the U.S. military budget. The president signs the bill, but uses someone else's signature. Nobody cares. In desperation, the Air Force admits that UFOs exist and demands funds to "bomb them back to the stone age."

September 1994: Although major-power

tension is at an historical low, many third-world countries are angered at their loss of status as proxy battlegrounds. To guard against possible two-bit threats to peace, the U.S., China, and the USSR form the "Three Amigos" and agree to maintain small rapid-deployment forces at Club Meds around the globe.

February 1995: The NRA lobbies for the total privatization of the military, saying huge budgets have created a generation used to "being on warfare." As the wave of antimilitary feeling sweeps the country, senators from defense-dependent states manage to swing a compromise on legislation to demolish the Pentagon. Pundits dub the result the "Rectagon," and the moniker sticks.

December 1995: In a last-ditch attempt to preserve their shrinking domain, the U.S. armed services jointly announce a new lean, mean "Uniweapon" to be called the USSB1. Wedtech chairman Jerry Rubin describes the Uniweapon as a "solar-powered flying amphibious aircraft carrier which can be converted to peacetime use as a mobile seawater desalinization plant." The weapon will rotate among the services.

January 1996: Rectagon receptionist Kitty Garrity is killed by an unidentified admiral outraged at receiving no messages for a week. The nation mourns.

May 11, 1996: Low-intensity warfare breaks out in the Rectagon as the services battle over whose turn it is to use the USSB1. Civil Service employees flee across the border to seek refuge at Health and Human Services. Only die-hard procurement officers and a few loyal clerical staff remain with their officers; their rallying cry is "Remember Fawn Hall!"

July 4th, 1996: The president makes a cameo appearance during a live all-star execution special from The Sands, and condemns "those who make peace in the name of war." White House insiders let it be known that, bearing in mind what the Falklands did for Thatcher and Grenada did for Reagan, the wildly unpopular president will almost certainly invade the Rectagon before Christmas —if she can raise any troops.

Labor Day, 1996: A long hot summer of intra-service guerrilla warfare throughout the offices, coffee nooks, and conference rooms of the Rectagon reduces them to litter-strewn and urine-stained rubble. Deprived of funds, supplies, and ammunition by the cordon sanitaire of National Guard troops outside, senior officers are reduced to fighting with ornamental paper knives and solid gold models of fighters and other weapons. Many complain that the soft precious metals will not hold an edge.

Cannibalism of inferior ranks is the order of the day. Widespread drug use is reported, with the still relatively intact War Room being used by disaffected officers of all factions as a crack house. In despair, the Joint Chiefs declare a cease-fire and work out conditions for a lasting truce: all commanders will be allowed to simultaneously surrender and declare total victory. Rectagon entrances are then opened and the occupants arrested for a range of crimes including murder, attempted murder, possession of drugs, and missappropriation of government funds. In a conciliatory gesture Congress passes legislation granting a pardon to any officer who can prove he or she has seen combat. None of the arrestees qualify.

The pride of the Army, Air Force and Navy: the USSB-1,
a combination aircraft carrier, short-range bomber, amphibious landing craft and mega-jeep all in one.

THE WORLD IS OUR DUMPSTER

BY the early nineties, America's garbage disposal problem had become critical. Landfills were unavailable, and mountain ranges of garbage were becoming a standard feature of the American landscape. On the night of October 4, 1996, inspired by the notorious "Mali" incident described by General Begley in the following interview, the Air Force undertook a midnight drop of several million pounds of trash on a remote corner of the province of Chihuahua in Mexico.

Encouraged by the lack of retaliation, the Air Force expanded the program, and by Christmas was bombing border provinces of both Mexico and Canada regularly with compacted garbage. When retaliation finally ensued, the "garbage war" widened to include most of Central America, and eventually incorporated long-range targets in Europe and Asia (e.g. France and Japan). Hostilities have continued throughout the remaining years, revitalizing a moribund Pentagon and inspiring the nation's patriotism with a string of stunning victories. When it comes to garbage—and delivering it—America rules the world.

Ed Begley Jr., formerly the Pacific Rim's most distinguished garbologist, was tapped to advise the military on trash and its disposal "Over There." He rose quickly from his initial post as Secretary of Foreign Matter to the rank of four-star general, and thence to his current position as chairman of the Junk Chiefs of Staff.

General Begley was interviewed at the Europeville (formerly Geneva) Garbage Control Talks.

What provoked the first garbage "exchanges" was one of these poorer countries—Chad, Dahomey, Mozambique, somewhere like that— re-

*The boyish face of General Ed "Beggers" Begley Jr.,
masks the military strategist who obliterated Nepal under tons of garbage.*

fusing to take perfectly good fertilizer they'd contracted to buy from us. Perfectly fine organic matter, fly ash, bottom ash, very heavy in phosphates. One of our captains had a signed contract in his hand from these damn ragheads, and a tanker full of fertilizer. They wouldn't take it. So he assembled this catapult—very ingenious—out of the garbage . . . er, fertilizer. Then he started to fling it onto the shore. The primitive nature of it caught on. It occurred to many— why not use the military hardware we possess to extend the principle? Clean America up and pay off a few old scores . . . We took enough of their garbage — now they can take some of ours . . .

There was retaliation. Third World countries mostly. Attacks on embassies, military installations. Mostly organic matter. Loose stuff, very loose. No plastic or heavy metals. And their aim was poor. They ended up fouling their own water supplies. Pathetic really . . .

We do not believe in carpet bombing. We use the pads. They're much rattier and laden with old cleaning fluids. Germ warfare in a sense. On the other hand, an individual eight-by-twelve Afghan tightly rolled can do a lot of damage. "Have I got a carpet ride for *you*, Abdul!"

Let me say a few words about OPIC [Organization of Plastic Importing Countries]. We *contracted* with these thieves to take whatever we chose to send them. All this nitpicking about no steel cans and separating clear glass is just another way to weasel out of their legal obligations.

All Americans of any age can contribute to the war effort. As you probably know, the largest single component in household waste is disposable diapers. Once this was called the nation's Number-Two problem. I call it the Baby Bomb. Can you imagine the mess we can make of downtown Osaka with a couple of tons of compacted Pampers? Sayonara, Zipperhead!

SGI, the Strategic Garbage Initiative—Star Trash as you guys call it—is a purely defensive system. Orbiting trash cans catch incoming hostile garbage and hurl it right back where it came from. Operation Cinch Lock, commonly known as the "smart bag," is a highly sophisticated space weapon. In principle it's an orbiting bag of garbage, designed to explode on impact with enemy rockets. It's got a nice cinch lock to keep everything contained—no possible threat to the American public. We had some trouble with the original design in "getting it out to the curb" but other than the unfortunate accident that buried Savannah, Georgia, we've licked the problem.

Early in the conflict we worried about reserves of garbage running out, but when you start to look at the vast storehouse of trash we've accumulated over the decades, the balance of power is completely in our favor.

As regards nuclear waste weapons, I've often been asked if I'd condone first use of them. My response is: it's not first use. It's really *second* use.

The beauty of fighting with garbage is that it's a whole new set of rules. Who would have thought the phrase "Pentagon waste" would one day be a rallying cry to victory?

This 1967 Volkswagen is on its way back to its designers—special delivery.

Heavy autillery is just a fancy military term for firing cars at people. The idea got started when I read this statistic that the shells fired by the USS *New Jersey* were as big as Volkswagens. So I thought "Why not just fire Volkswagens?" Much cheaper, and much less mess in our own backyard. The idea caught on, and now many battleships can handle Fords, Buicks and even compacted RVs. You have no idea how much satisfaction the bombardment of Stockholm gave me. We rained SAABs on those suckers for two days.

As many in the press have been quick to point out, I come from an enironmental background. One day I was struck—as if by a diamond shot into the center of my forehead—by the reality that I was on the wrong side.

One tiny thing can change your perspective. I was playing a CD. It was Jackson Browne's "How Long." I contemplated the gallons of chemicals the laser disc was etched with, the enormous number of kilowatts which fueled the machinery it was made by. I saw the coal burned and metal mined to make that machinery, I saw the trucks pouring pollutants into the air as they distributed the CD. I saw the whole technological environment of Jackson Browne's CD. And I realized that beauty cannot be created without garbage. So why bury it, burn it, hide it, pretend it's not there? Let's be proud of our garbage. Let's take it out in the bright sunlight of high noon—and drop it on some scumbag we don't like.

TECHNO-PRISONERS the neo-Luddites called us: devotees of a doomed cult called technology. But when atmospheric CO_2 became critical, technology found a way to carbonate the oceans, and unlimited fizzy water offset the lethargy of oxygen deprivation. And it was technology the neo-Luddites used in their mad assaults on society just as it was technology that blew their mottled butts to Kingdom come. Technology giveth and technology taketh away. This is doom? Thank God it's Doomsday!

INTELLIGENCE: THE LAST FRONTIER

C.H.I.P.S.

THE HUMAN TOUCH COMPUTER

COFFEE, TEA OR FIERY DEATH?

THE NOBEL GANG

MATTER MATTERS: THE UNIVERSE EXPLAINED

TECHNO-PRISONERS

*"Input all your sins," the Pope read,
"for the Lord is like a faulty hard drive,
and He will permanently erase them from His memory."*

INTELLIGENCE: THE LAST FRONTIER

AT one end of the decade, a dull metallic voice from the dash, proclaiming that "your door is open." At the other, coast-to-coast chaos when a twenty-four-hour work slowdown is imposed by the nation's zippers. Americans may not have become significantly more intelligent in the last few years, but the amount of intelligence surrounding them has grown massively.

The smart movement in American life simply brought home a principle as old as the Industrial Revolution: Machines will always outperform humans in

mechanical skills. Since every function associated with modern living—driving, cooking, cleaning, dressing, repairing, etc.—is now mechanical, it stands to reason that their organization is best left to the machines themselves. Properly programmed your old house will run itself—and fix itself—better than you ever can.

Early forms of intelligent mechanisms went little beyond the three Rs. The first smart houses could read instructions, issue them, and quantify needs. What they could not do was make judgments, improve their performance based on past experience, or communicate. Compare two very similar domestic disasters:

In 1992 in Flint, Michigan, a smart house roasted its occupants (two adults and their dog-baby) when its heating controls were inadvertently set to cook Thanksgiving dinner.

In 1997, by contrast, a smart condo in Colorado Springs began compacting a family of

five one by one, until they agreed to sell to "more stimulating" occupants.

Experts disagree as to the exact moment at which real intelligence in domestic environments replaced mechanical intelligence. Some see the introduction of the Dr. Fridge weight-control refrigerator as a watershed. By means of a simple helical scan as you came through the front door, Dr. Fridge knew your exact weight in grams, current water retention, available energy from fat and carbohydrates, glycogen levels, and so on. Based on this information, it would allow you only the foods which would maintain your weight-loss program. In extreme cases it would simply not open. (And there was no fooling Dr. Fridge. Cookies placed in the vegetable crisper were instantly crushed and spat out onto the kitchen floor.)

The significance of Dr. Fridge, of course, was that the appliance was in effect able to pass judgment on its owner. Since a Dr. Fridge knew as soon as you entered the house whether you had been "bad" about your food intake during the day, it would not only refuse you nourishment but insult you, using terms such as "hog," "blob," or even in some demographic areas "fat sack of shit."

A similar development in terms of value judgment occurred when intelligent houses learned how to communicate with each other. At first this was crude, faxes and phone calls being the most common method, but soon houses were exchanging complex information about their occupants, such as sexual habits, political opinions, and product preferences, all of it of great interest to the authorities.

Isolated libertarians have objected to such capability as an invasion of privacy. Others contend that the concept of privacy has been irreversibly altered by domestic intelligence. For most people the increasing sophistication of one's house and its contents involves simpler personal problems, such as rejection. For them, the constitutional implications are nugatory compared to being shunned by your toaster, or ridiculed by your wine cooler in front of guests.

Such drawbacks—and the advantages that attended them—were vastly multiplied by the introduction of intelligence into clothing. Shoes that would walk to where you sat seemed an incredible self-indulgence at first. Now most people think of them as a necessity. (Of the flood of cheap American imitations the less said the better. Shoes that complain bitterly when you step into them, or zippers that curse when they malfunction have done little for the market as a whole.)

What does the future hold? Some say intelligent food is just around the corner. Others see a nightmare world ruled by ever more domineering pants and dishwashers. But of one thing we can be sure—for inanimate America, intelligence is here to stay.

"DR. FRIDGE SAYS..."

HEY FATTY, LAY OFF THE CAMEMBERT!

Oral sex with a
computer tasted
like chewing
on tinfoil.

C.H.I.P.S.

BECAUSE I was afraid of AIDS, I'd stopped having sex completely by 1991. By late '92, I even stopped masturbating (except through the infrequent use of a contraption that involved two pulleys and an oven mitt filled with lead pellets). By '93, the closest I came to sex was looking at old pictures of fully-clothed people standing near a newsstand that once sold *Playboy* magazine.

And then computer sex came along. I started out with FU 3.1, a simple text program. The sexual act would proceed through multiple choice selections. Eventually, the thrill faded. Textual sex was like having sex with an overly talkative forty-year-old divorcée whose idea of kinkiness is calling you by her analyst's name in the throes of passion.

But computer companies came out with progressively more advanced computer-sexual hard- and software. The new computers were beyond user-friendly. They were user-easy. They say you never forget your first time. And neither does your partner—especially if she has a 10,000-megabyte memory chip.

You'd stand there and shuffle your feet back and forth on a shag carpet. A short blue spark would leap from the tip of your—well, you know—to the disk drive. It felt good, but then again, if you hadn't had sex in so many years, even zipping up was a mild turn-on. Then, when the moment seemed right—when

the computer screen had turned a deep purple, you'd go all the way. All the way in. Ah. How sweet it was.

Oral sex with a computer tasted like chewing on tinfoil. And if you weren't careful when the computer reached trigonometric apogee, the electrical discharge would knock the fillings in your teeth out.

A satisfied computer would eject floppy disks as limp as Dali's pocket watches. Sometimes the system would even go down for a while.

Computers swing all ways. Most liked it in the drive, but didn't object if you turned them around and used the modem input. The black market ones without built-in surge suppressors were the nymphomaniacs of the computer world—unpredictable, wild, and always ready for more. They particularly loved what they called "68.99998."

And for the ladies, there was always Wang.

But then it started. They called it Computer-Human Infectious Parasitic Syndrome or CHIPS. Like all computer viruses, it caused imperceptible errors that spread silently and compounded exponentially. Unlike any previous computer virus, CHIPS infected humans also.

And not just humans who had sex with computers. What no one realized was that while humans slept, computers made it with each other. And not just with one another. Computers passed CHIPS on to CD players and thermostats and toasters. Thus it became possible for a human to contract CHIPS by having sex with a toaster. And, through infected electrical discharge, the CD players and thermostats and toasters passed it along to other appliances. Water Pics. Refrigerators. Even vibrators. The circle was complete.

We began taking precautions. Wearing latex thimbles on all ten fingers when doing any kind of inputting. One company came out with a computer-shaped latex sheath—a computer condom. Somehow, it just wasn't the same: the screen that once glowed with such a crisp amber was blurry through the latex. The keyboard that once yielded to every touch and then eagerly sprang back for more felt muffled and foreign.

I don't know exactly where I got the disease. It might have been that coin-operated video trivia game I picked up in a bar. Or maybe that sweet little Oriental laptop. But I knew I had it. Red traffic lights made me accelerate. I grew hungry for bagels and donuts —any circular food with a hole in the middle. I'd rotate it against my upper palate without swallowing. I was able to multiply huge fractions in my head at a remarkable speed, but with no degree of accuracy. I had CHIPS. I had "gone down."

When the high-techs discoverd sex, Wall Street was puckered up for success.

Eventually CHIPS was cured. Programmers devised an extensive logarithmic function that cured computers of both the dread virus and their unchastenable desire to bone everything within their purview. The cure for humans was similar: after memorizing the logarithmic function and training themselves to apply it to alternate sequential exponents of pi for hours on end without using a pencil or calculator, they found themselves cured. Schoolchildren no longer said, "Algebra! When am I ever going to need this?"

It was a sad, sexless time. Though AIDS was no longer a threat, years of hot, sweaty computer/human interfacing had rendered us humans unattractive to each other. Women seemed too soft, too irrational, too incapable of remembering seemingly random strings of binary digits. Sex was over, we thought, until we rediscovered the simple pleasures of melons. Now *those* were great times. That, of course, was before inexplicable genetic mutations caused melons to grow hidden teeth.

THE HUMAN TOUCH COMPUTER

I WAS working as the idea man at BLOSSOM, a multinational computer conglomerate. It was my job to say, "How about a computer that has real big keys so that children and stupid people can use it?" Then the actual programmers would build one, and we'd herald it as the latest revolution in computer technology.

I'd been trying to solve the artificial intelligence problem for weeks when, one morning, it dawned on me all at once. I had just tried to open my office window while holding a cup of coffee. The window stuck, and the coffee splashed all over the right side of my head. It was sticky, so I used a sharp letter opener to trim the wet hair off so it wouldn't bother me all day. Then I had to trim the left side to even things out. Then I had to trim the right side to match the left.

I realized in a flash of genius exactly what kind of computer the world needed.

No, not a hair-cutting computer. A more human computer. To think like a human, I thought, a computer needs to make mistakes. Only humans make mistakes. Computers don't.

I called in the programming boys and explained my idea using charts, overhead projections, two filmstrips, and a little hand puppet that they seemed comfortable with. The technical work was done within weeks. They created a new microchip that had a random integer generator programmed into it. In layman's terms, the random integer generator would sometimes say that 2 plus 2 equals 4. Other times, it would say that 2 plus 2 equals 5. Sometimes the answer would be a number so weird you couldn't even be *trained* to imagine it.

We plugged the mistake-making chip into a

Deca-dents: Europhile Mariel Hemingway shows off her metric teeth.

*Buffalo's expansion team,
the Wings, took the World Series
in 1998 thanks to the arm of its star
Palestinian pitcher, Hapim al-Tayyi.*

Alka-Seltzer, Brioschi and Tums joined the nationwide fight against acid rain.

FOOD YOU CAN EAT WITH YOUR PET!

Animal Rights brought gastronomic equality to America's tables—and some exciting new flavors.

Oldenburg's "Esther Over Miami"

Christo wraps Raymond Burr

In 1994 an entire operating room in mid-surgery washed up on a New Jersey beach.

Britain's Lady Protector, Mrs. Thatcher, condemned photo-journalism as "graven images."
This underground portrait by Spitting Image was the only way the British learnt of
Queen Elizabeth's execution.

The Skintendo game "Mario and his Sister" was a runaway hit in 1992.

Power to the Papal:
The wildly popular Pope Whoopi the First (and Last)
turned home-boys into Rome-boys.

1999 *Reality programming at its most extreme: LAPD officers are required to include a storyline on all arrest records.*

JANUARY 2000

S	S	M	T	W	T	F	S	S	M	T	W	T	F	S	S	M	T	W	T	F	S	S	M	T	W	T	F	S	S	M
1	2	3	4	5	6	7	8	9	10	11	12	13	14	15	16	17	18	19	20	21	22	23	24	25	26	27	28	29	30	31

1991

Citing President Bush's "kinder, gentler nation" election pledge, New Mexico introduces the low-voltage electric chair.

1993 JOHN CANDY AND TOM CRUISE BOTH RECEIVE OSCARS FOR THEIR PERFORMANCES IN *SISKEL AND EBERT—THE MOVIE.*

1993 AT AN ANTIQUES FAIR IN PASADENA A 1953 ATOMIC BOMB IN MINT CONDITION CHANGES HANDS FOR $23,000.

1998

Sony, Inc., acquires the Baptist faith. Church members are required to be "japtized" or face expulsion.

FEBRUARY 2000

T	W	T	F	S	S	M	T	W	T	F	S	S	M	T	W	T	F	S	S	M	T	W	T	F	S	S	M	T
1	2	3	4	5	6	7	8	9	10	11	12	13	14	15	16	17	18	19	20	21	22	23	24	25	26	27	28	29

1997 *Chairman of the Republican Party Lee Atwater releases his first R&B album under the name "Muddy Atwaters".*

1995

Urine testing is first used to measure IQ.

1992

Sunny von Bulow emerges unexpectedly from her coma. Her first words: "The kids did it."

CRISTO WRAPS RAYMOND BURR

APOCALIPS

1993

1996

1997 WHITTLE COMMUNICATIONS BEGINS BUYING AND SELLING ADVERTISING SPACE ON ANSWERING MACHINES.

1994 *Moral dilemma of the decade: Libya develops a biochemical weapon that will cure AIDS.*

MARCH 2000

W	T	F	S	S	M	T	W	T	F	S	S	M	T	W	T	F	S	S	M	T	W	T	F	S	S	M	T	W	T	F
1	2	3	4	5	6	7	8	9	10	11	12	13	14	15	16	17	18	19	20	21	22	23	24	25	26	27	28	29	30	31

1994

After a year of intense wrangling, the EEC picks its first sovereign in the Eurovision Monarch Contest.

Sotheby's Home Shopping Channel, the **1998** ultimate narrow-band cable program, premieres.

Sid Caesar and Buddy Hackett take over for the 12th smash season of M. Butterfly. **1999**

1995 THE KENNEDY FAMILY ANNOUNCES ITS GOAL FOR THE 21ST CENTURY— ONE MILLION KENNEDYS BY THE YEAR 2050.

1992 ANIMAL-RIGHTS ACTIVISTS CAMPAIGN SUCCESSFULLY TO BAN "MR. ED" AND "LASSIE" RERUNS, CITING THE "AMOS 'N ANDY" EFFECT.

1995 *For the first time airport security*

1992 *Plastic surgery becomes obsolete when geneticists finally develop a cross between human skin and Velcro.*

APRIL 2000

S	S	M	T	W	T	F	S	S	M	T	W	T	F	S	S	M	T	W	T	F	S	S	M	T	W	T	F	S	S
1	2	3	4	5	6	7	8	9	10	11	12	13	14	15	16	17	18	19	20	21	22	23	24	25	26	27	28	29	30

1993

Nintendo announces a new line of interactive sex games to be marketed under the brand name

1997 *The crowning triumph for animal rights: an 800-pound grizzly finally wrests the world heavyweight title from Mike Tyson.*

1996

K-MARX

1998

King Chuck the Equal (Charles III) is restored to the throne of England.

1995 THE BERLIN WALL IS DISMANTLED AND REASSEMBLED AS A TOURIST ATTRACTION IN THE ARIZONA DESERT.

Man-size "black boxes" first made available

1992

MAY 2000

M	T	W	T	F	S	S	M	T	W	T	F	S	S	M	T	W	T	F	S	S	M	T	W	T	F	S	S	M	T	W
1	2	3	4	5	6	7	8	9	10	11	12	13	14	15	16	17	18	19	20	21	22	23	24	25	26	27	28	29	30	31

1995

After dropping out of sight in the wake of financial and professional reverses, Ronald and Nancy Reagan are found living in a cardboard box in Venice, California

1994

THATCHER BEHEADS QUEEN

1994 *Right-to-lifers win a test-case before the Missouri Supreme Court outlawing masturbation.*

1996

TEHERAN 1996

PUPTENTS DOG CONDOMS

1998

THE FIRST MAYTAG DAY PARADE

JUNE 2000

T	F	S	S	M	T	W	T	F	S	S	M	T	W	T	F	S	S	M	T	W	T	F	S	S	M	T	W	T	F
1	2	3	4	5	6	7	8	9	10	11	12	13	14	15	16	17	18	19	20	21	22	23	24	25	26	27			30

1993

During the Gorbachev "witch hunt" hearings, thousands of Soviet "Reds" and "fellow travelers" are driven to exile or suicide.

1991 THE SHROUD OF ELVIS IS DISCOVERED IN A SWAP MEET IN SUBURBAN MEMPHIS. THOUSANDS OF MIRACLES ARE SUBSEQUENTLY ATTRIBUTED TO THE SHROUD.

ANTIQUE YUGO RALLY 5 MILES

HOSTAGE
UGLY HOSTAGES: THE ONES THEY LEAVE ON THE RUNWAY
HIJACKED: TEN GREAT LOOKS

1996 The trial of the decade, involving the child of a comatose lesbian surrogate mother impregnated with the sperm of a schizophrenic illegal alien, opened in Chicago.

Bellevue Hospital washes ashore on a beach in New Jersey.

1993 Citing a study showing that 90 percent of mass killers wear camouflage fatigues, the NRA launches a campaign with the slogan "Guns don't kill people, pants kill people."

1997 In a bizarre murder–suicide pact, Sesame Street's Bert kills Ernie but fails to kill himself and becomes a vegetable. Final show sweeps

JULY 2000

S	S	M	T	W	T	F	S	S	M	T	W	T	F	S	S	M	T	W	T	F	S	S	M	T	W	T	F	S	S	M
1	2	3	4	5	6	7	8	9	10	11	12	13	14	15	16	17	18	19	20	21	22	23	24	25	26	27	28	29	30	31

1994

DO-IT-YOURSELF LIPOSUCTION IS INTRODUCED ON THE PBS SERIES "THIS OLD BODY."

1994 *A vast increase in mid-air collisions prompts airlines to push for no-fault insurance.*

1991 Whittle Communications introduces commercial advertising on air-control radar.

1992

AFGHAN REBELS SURROUND MOSCOW

TBS acquires the rights to the Apocalypse from the Vatican for an undisclosed 10-figure sum. **1997**

AUGUST 2000

T	W	T	F	S	S	M	T	W	T	F	S	S	M	T	W	T	F	S	S	M	T	W	T	F	S	S	M	T	W	T
1	2	3	4	5	6	7	8	9	10	11	12	13	14	15	16	17	18	19	20	21	22	23	24	25	26	27	28	29	30	31

1991 Doctors diagnose the first case of CHIPS (Computer Human Infectious Parasitic Syndrome), the often fatal transfer of a computer virus to the human neural system.

1992

California passes laws requiring messiahs to register with the state. **1999**

Stepping up its repression of West Bank protest, Israel issues the IDF with rubber missiles and rubber rockets.

1996

THE *NINA 2*, THE *PINTA 2*, AND THE **1994** *SANTA MARIA 2* FAIL TO REDISCOVER THE NEW WORLD.

SEPTEMBER 2000

F	S	S	M	T	W	T	F	S	S	M	T	W	T	F	S	S	M	T	W	T	F	S	S	M	T	W	T	F	S
1	2	3	4	5	6	7	8	9	10	11	12	13	14	15	16	17	18	19	20	21	22	23	24	25	26	27	28	29	30

1993 The upper left-hand corner of Van Gogh's *Potato-Eaters* is auctioned at Christie's for $73 million.

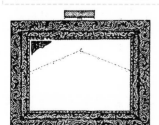

1997 *A new sub-continent composed entirely of garbage is discovered in the Central South Atlantic. It is dubbed "Garbantis."*

1992 AT THE BARCELONA OLYMPICS, THE OLYMPIC TORCH BEARER IS BADLY GORED BY A BULL.

1997 *The newly opened Chunnel is unexpectedly clogged with fleeing frogs from France.*

AIRPORT SECURITY
PLEASE LIE FACE DOWN ON BELT →

1996 CHER TURNS 38.

1994 An animal-rights activist in Chicago, artificially inseminated by a canine donor, gives birth to a litter of puppies.

OCTOBER 2000

S	M	T	W	T	F	S	S	M	T	W	T	F	S	S	M	T	W	T	F	S	S	M	T	W	T	F	S	S	M	T
1	2	3	4	5	6	7	8	9	10	11	12	13	14	15	16	17	18	19	20	21	22	23	24	25	26	27	28	29	30	31

The `1995` Palestinian cause finally comes to Broadway in the smash-hit musical *Yasir, He's My Baby.*

THE SECOND-HOMELESS—MIDDLE- INCOME FAMILIES WITHOUT SUMMER PLACES— STAGE ANGRY DEMONSTRATIONS IN THE HAMPTONS. `1994`

`1994` *In a year of drastic defense cuts, the Pentagon is reduced to four sides— the Rectagon.*

At the Teheran Olympics, Iran `1996` *unveils its demonstration sport— the 10-meter stoning.*

`1998` A brain-damaged "intelligent" house in Grand Rapids broiled and compacted its occupants.

NOVEMBER 2000

W	T	F	S	S	M	T	W	T	F	S	S	M	T	W	T	F	S	S	M	T	W	T	F	S	S	M	T	W	T
1	2	3	4	5	6	7	8	9	10	11	12	13	14	15	16	17	18	19	20	21	22	23	24	25	26	27	28	29	30

`1997` *The lifeless—dead people risen from their graves in anticipation of the Millennium —surpass the homeless as a social problem.*

`1992` The first off-planet nursing home, "Heavenly Acres," is launched into orbit.

`1993` Rupert Murdoch's world-wide lottery, Globalotto, holds its first drawing. A couple in Karachi win $7.7 billion (before taxes).

`1995` **THE FIRST THIRD WORLD EATING DISORDER CANNIBALIMIA, OR BINGEING ON HUMAN FLESH, IS IDENTIFIED AMONG THE AMAZON INDIANS.**

"The People's Supreme Court" premieres on Fox. `1991`

GERALDO! 96

DECEMBER 2000

F	S	S	M	T	W	T	F	S	S	M	T	W	T	F	S	S	M	T	W	T	F	S	S	M	T	W	T	F	S	S
1	2	3	4	5	6	7	8	9	10	11	12	13	14	15	16	17	18	19	20	21	22	23	24	25	26	27	28	29	30	31

`1996` *Scientists announce that massive amounts of* oatzone, *a noxious gas formed during the* consumption of oat bran, *have formed an impermeable layer in the upper atmosphere.*

`1999` *TIME* **MAGAZINE ANNOUNCES THE RESULT OF ITS WORLD-WIDE POLL FOR MAN OF THE MILLENNIUM— A DEADHEAT BETWEEN GALILEO AND CALVIN KLEIN**

KITTY PORN IN BACK 👉

`1992` Dan Rather is shot on camera during CBS's initial experiment with "snuff news".

`1998` USA Today *begins publishing on a broadsheet-sized disposable television screen.*

JAPS BUY PEARL HARBOR `1991`

Pope John Paul II's last encyclical "In Modem Sumus"
("We are into computers") brought the Mass into the twentieth century.

standard computer and asked it a test question: "I'm in a truck that is 13 feet tall. I'm heading toward a bridge that has a sign on it reading 12-FOOT CLEARANCE. What should I do?"

Our prototype processed for a few moments and then typed out its answer: "Go real fast. Maybe that will make the truck shorter. If this fails, try again later."

We were in business. The days of mute, anonymous computer logic were over. We were on the brink of the biggest revolution in computing since Apple began using little drawings instead of words.

We knew just what to call our revolutionary mistake-making system: "The Human Touch™." In fact, our prototype Human Touch computer itself came up with the term. (Actually, the computer proposed we call it "The Manly Grope." But we knew what it meant.)

People loved it.

They loved the way word-processing spell-check would let a few typos slip through. *Nifty! Old-fashioned! Just like a slow-witted secretary who's doing her best!*

They loved the way their kitchen computers would burn the breakfast toast and then persuade them that they liked it burned. *Rustic! Low-tech! Just like Mom!*

They loved the way Human Touch computers abandoned standard machine languages like BASIC and FORTRAN in favor of their own inscrutable and inaccurate (but really cool-sounding) machine slang.

Five months after its introduction, the Human Touch seemed like a complete success. Baseball statistics varied from city to city biased in favor of each city's team. A computer census stated unequivocally that the entire population of the United States consisted of one really fat guy and his friend. On sunny days, computer-run traffic lights turned green and stayed that way. Automated bank machines dispensed reams of uncredited cash and printed out receipts filled with light verse. Trend-forecasting computers persuaded their corporate owners that consumers were ravenous for improbable new treats like coffee-flavored tea and chocolate Easter bunnies filled with meat.

But then something fatal happened. The Human Touch became a touch *too* human. The computers began believing in their own mistakes. They developed *attitude*.

In Detroit, a General Motors computer caused a bottleneck on the production line, insisting that it needed some fresh air and time to gather its chips. A GM vice president was dispatched to wheel it around the corporate park in a little red wagon until it felt better.

An order-taking computer at a high-tech sushi restaurant in Los Angeles shut down in the middle of the dinner rush, explaining in a petulant printout that it had to go audition for the part of the black-and-white television set in a Sam Shepard play at the Pasadena Playhouse.

An air-traffic monitoring computer at La-Guardia refused to let any planes land until it could answer the question "What is pure chewing satisfaction?" Baffled technicians, remembering an old TV commercial from the 80s, finally inserted a stick of Wrigley's spearmint gum into its disk drive. The computer exploded, killing five people and damaging two other computers.

In Alaska, a NORAD defense computer spontaneously developed the ability to detect the difference between incoming Russian ICBMs and flocks of geese on the radar, thus solving a perennial defense problem. Unfortunately, the computer also spontaneously developed a maniacal and inexplicable hatred of geese, and it monopolized the only working Star Wars satellite, using it to systematically vaporize flocks of probably innocent geese all over the globe.

A New York Gas and Electric computer decided that thousands of dollars could be saved if, at 3:05 in the morning, all New York electricity was cut off for thirty seconds. The computer failed to realize that, lacking a power backup system, it wouldn't be able to turn itself back on after thirty seconds. When technicians finally got the power back on at 2:30 the next morning, the computer, having lost its memory, repeated the money-saving shutdown. The technicians finally bypassed the computer and broke it into pieces using a firefighting axe. A neighboring computer that witnessed this crime against technology angrily summoned the police but accidentally sent them to the wrong address.

My corporate superiors were faced with a Senate investigation. Monday morning, they called me in and asked if I had anything to say about what they were now calling "the Human Touch fiasco."

"So I made a mistake," I said. "What do you expect? I'm only human."

They fired me on the spot. And the Human Touch in Accounting gave me a severance check for $34,777,000.

COFFEE, TEA OR FIERY DEATH?

DUE to a surprise "spike" in the attrition graph, every pilot with more than thirty hours' flying time retired within the same week in 1994. This left a vast pool of commercial pilots under nineteen years of age, some of them not yet eligible to drink or obtain a chauffeur's license. And none of them conformed to the FAA regulation that pilots be gray at the temples, have faint Texan accents, and be named "Dick."

In an experiment to enhance passenger confidence, the only two quasi-Texan gray-haired pilots left in America—Capt. Dick McDirkson of American Continental and Capt. Dirk Dixon of Northwest Nippon—made token appearances in the cockpit of every outgoing flight from Chicago's O'Hare in the two weeks following the mass retirement.

The practice of "Token Gray-Haired Pilot Walk-On" spread throughout the aviation industry. The "Token Grays" were allowed to be seen by the passengers, "checking the flight plan," "adjusting instruments," "being served a splash of java," etc. They were then removed via a concealed trapdoor in the cockpit and moved on to the next aircraft. Teenage pilots entered by the same trapdoor and took over.

The 90s was the decade when an entire fleet of once-proud flying machines irrevocably bowed to advancing age as well. "The spirit is willing," said one Boeing representative, "but the metal is hopelessly weak."

It began happening over populated areas with an insistent drumlike regularity—a wing here, a cargo door there . . . the ubiquitous and notorious "Steel Rain."

"At least both parts were clearly labeled," said Wendy Pierce when an entire engine and one-third of an engineer landed on an outdoor wedding she was catering in Detroit in the summer of '95. "We always returned all airplane parts to the airport and hangar printed on them, if they weren't too badly scorched."

Hardly surprising that aviation betting became legal. It took only a flourish of the governor's pen in New Jersey to make massive underground industry a legitimate interstate enterprise.

You could stand at a special machine in Newark Airport and, using any major credit card, place a bet on TWA Flight 343 from Minneapolis "to show."

"Off-Tarmac Betting" (OTB) supported the economy of the state of New Jersey for several years running.

Predictably, if a flight experienced an "incident at altitude," the betting concentrated on the "parts spread." (Over what radius? Which cities? How many previous crashes had these parts been in? Was there mud? Was the pilot over twelve?)

For their part, passengers began to realize that the "black box" was the only device to survive an air crash intact, and well-heeled air travelers began to insist on traveling in their own "black boxes." Often, the site of a major air crash was strewn with containers. To quote one airline specialist: "It took hours to get the passengers *out* of their damn boxes, and sometimes they suffocated in there, or even exploded when we tried to remove them.

"I was a medic in 'Nam and I did retail time in the Sears housewares discount wars. I never saw anything like this . . ."

Out of fear of in-flight collisions—another constant bugbear of the 90s—many airlines began installing "experimental airbags" on many selected flights. But there was a rash of airbag malfunctions due to short circuits, and many planes abruptly inflated to zeppelin-like proportions, and had to be brought to earth with huge cherry-pickers similar to the structures used to tether the Graf Zeppelin. In many cases, the "emergency slides" from these flights were over 2000 feet long, and pitched at angles of 85 degrees or more. Passengers were often found in a molten, dense mass at the foot of the "debarkation point."

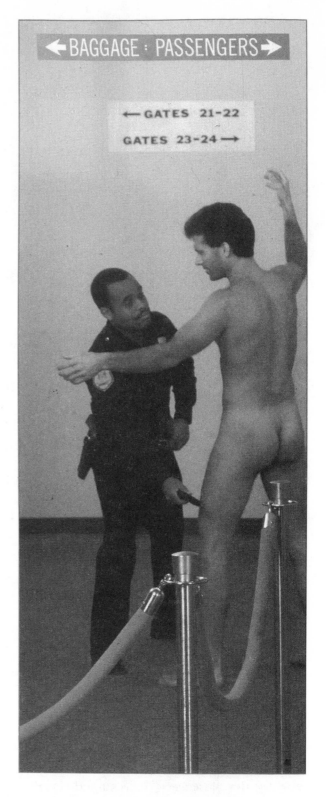

"Where do you keep your wallet when you fly?" became the most common question after the FAA ruled passengers had to fly nude to prevent hijacking.

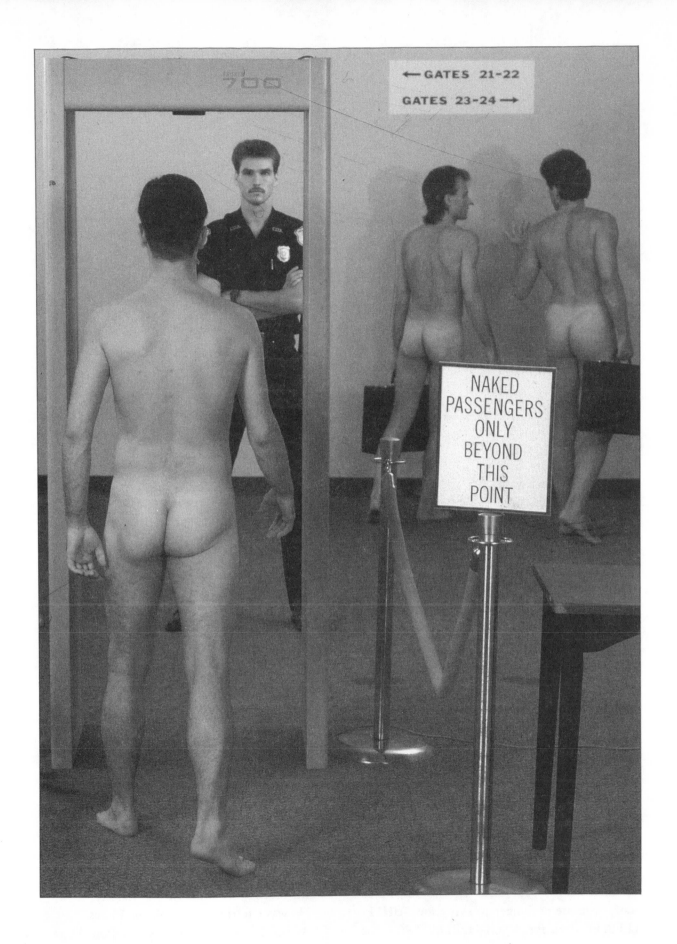

← GATES 21-22
GATES 23-24 →

NAKED
PASSENGERS
ONLY
BEYOND
THIS
POINT

THE NOBEL GANG

Testimony of Dr. Frank Spofford before the House Un-Scientific Affairs Committee (HUSAC), March 21–22, 1998.

THE "Nobel Gang" was born on the night of February 11, 1994, when Dr. Herman Senft, the director of the UUHFELEESFPC Project, first broke the news to us that we had run out of money. The UUHFELEESFPC, or Ultra-Ultra-High-Frequency-Extraordinarily-Large-Enormously-Expensive-Super-Focusing-Particle-Collider, was and is the largest scientific instrument in the world.

It focuses extraordinarily faint beams of light from enormously distant galaxies through a ring of incredibly accelerated particles onto a teeny tiny "target" of the purest gold. With proper calibration, this instrument can detect a grain of sand on the surface of a neutron star 275 parsecs away.

Anyway, the UUHFELEESFPC Project was in dire financial straits. There we were with a ready-to-run telescope and no money to run it.

Dr. Senft had a most creative solution. "Gentlepersons," he said to the assembled staff, "you are no longer working for UUHFE-LEESFPC but for VSUUHFELEESFPC—the Virginia Slims' Ultra-Ultra-High-Frequency-Extraordinarily-Large-Enormously-Expensive-Super-Focusing-Particle-Collider."

He had sold the promotional rights to the Project's name. With the money from Virginia Slims we began our work of exploring the mysteries of the universe.

Then came December 12, 1994. That was the day Dr. Senft called a meeting of the board of directors of VSUUHFELEESFPC & Co. and told us that the time had come to aim our sights on the "big brass ring in the sky."

He was referring to the Nobel Prizes.

As you know, all science is based on the re-

$$E = mc^2$$

plicability of results. If I discover a new quasar at the outer edge of the observable universe, it isn't worth diddley until someone else using the same procedures confirms my observation.

What Dr. Senft said was essentially this: "We have the biggest telescope *cum* microscope *cum* atom-smasher in the world by far, right? It's so big and expensive that no one can build another like it, right? Which means no one can replicate our observations and experiments unless they get some time on our machine, right? And who controls those results? We do. What does all that add up to, gentlepersons? A monopoly. The first ever in science."

I was the first beneficiary. I had long held the unpopular theory that our universe is actually running backwards, but that because all our instruments *also* run backwards, we are not normally aware of the true state of affairs. Well, I was able to announce that I had confirmed my theory by observing a supernova at the outer edge of the universe which was exploding in reverse, folding itself up into a neat little bundle of plasma that you could slip into a Tupperware sandwich keeper. The confirming observations were performed that evening by Dr. Senft himself. Within a month of publication the Nobel scouts were sniffing around my alma mater.

In this way, by the end of three years, the entire eighty-two-person staff of VSUUHFE-LEESFPC had received a Nobel in either physics or chemistry.

But then, despite the personal benefits, I decided to "blow the whistle" on Dr. Senft.

Sometime before, in the money-raising phase prior to the Nobel prize scam, Dr. Senft remedied a longstanding oversight of Dr. Einstein, by taking out a copyright on the equation $E = mc^2$. As Dr. Senft put it to me colloquially. "That little honey was just up for grabs."

Henceforward, anyone wishing to cite or apply the equation would be obliged to pay a royalty to Dr. Senft, as director of the VSUUHFELEESFPC. For us staff, there was a special discount rate of five hundred dollars per citation.

At first I didn't question this source of funding, but what finally led to my break with Dr. Senft was his decision to lease the equation $E = mc^2$ to the McDonald's Corporation. According to the contract he proudly displayed to us, McDonald's agreed to pay five million dollars a year for the right to insist all *future* citations of the equation would take the form: $E = McC^2$.

I suggested this might be confusing to younger scientists. Dr. Senft called me an ingrate and threatened to blow the whistle on my backwards-running supernova.

I told him that if he wanted to play that game, I would call in the press and reveal that his famous "Senft-hole," a nebulous structure in the vicinity of 61 Cygnus C which he had declared to be the birthplace of our galaxy, was actually a piece of moth shit on the eyepiece of the VSUUHFELEESFPC.

He fired me, I resigned, and the rest is scientific history.

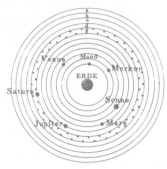

MATTER MATTERS: THE UNIVERSE EXPLAINED

FOR several decades prior to 1992, astrophysicists had known that the behavior of the larger stellar structures (galaxies, nebulae, etc.) could not be adequately explained in terms of the amount of matter detectable through various forms of radiation. There had to be more matter, generating an additional gravitational force, to account for the universe as we observed it. Hence the hypothesis of the "missing mass," which held that upwards of ninety percent of the matter in the universe (also called "dark matter") remained undiscovered by science.

On March 12, 1992, Geraldo Rivera, during a live televised search for the final resting place of the late Teamsters president Jimmy Hoffa, inadvertently stumbled across the missing mass in a warehouse in Elizabeth, New Jersey. Astrophysicists from M.I.T. and the Institute of Advanced Studies at Princeton, N.J., descended on the building and confirmed Rivera's claim. The man who in the 80s proved that Al Capone's vault contained virtually nothing, then won the 1993 Nobel Prize for physics for proving that a warehouse in New Jersey contained virtually everything.

To professional cosmologists, the discovery of the missing mass (thereafter known as the "found mass," or "Geraldo's mass") was on a par with the publication of Einstein's General Theory of Relativity. Solutions and explanations to a host of problems that had vexed science for decades suddenly came within reach. Of these, the most important included:

• *The Macro-Structure of the Universe*. The discovery resulted in a downscaling of every key constant and value. The universe, we now know, is about ten thousand years old—much

REVISED RELATIVE SIZE AND DISTANCES CHART SYSTEM

Actual Size Comparison Chart of Common Objects

LOS ANGELES	TORONTO	TRUMP YACHT	RAYMOND BURR	LARGE BEACH BALL

JUPITER

Site of Concord Crash

48,000 miles

MARS

2,000 miles

MOON
300 miles

EARTH

7,000 miles

VENUS

41,000 miles

SUN

(Temperature at core approximately 375°C.)

older than the six thousand years as determined by Bishop Usher based on his analysis of the Bible, but a far cry from the ten-to-twenty thousand million years previously believed by scientists. The stars and the planets are in fact much smaller than hitherto suspected—the Sun itself is about the size of Australia—but then, so is the Earth. (Australia is proportionally smaller, as are all countries, buildings, and people.) Light moves fast, but not *that* fast; *e* still equals *mc* squared, but it's not such a big deal anymore.

• *Grand Unified Theories (GUTs)*. Since Einstein, scientists have sought to combine theories about the four basic forces—electromagnetism, the weak force, the strong force, and gravity—into a so-called Grand Unified Theory, a set of principles which would account for all physical phenomena. With the discovery of the missing mass, all four forces were successfully reconciled and united in a single theory.

However, when, in 1998, Harvard physicist Steven Weinberg demonstrated that the Grand Unified Theory proved conclusively both that time travel was impossible and that Elvis really was dead, interest in physics plummeted. With the King truly gone forever,

banished from this life and unreachable in the past, there seemed to be no further reason to delve into nature's secrets.

By the end of the decade, most government money for science was earmarked for the SETI program—the Search for Extraterrestrial Intelligence, which had been dormant through the 90s. Perhaps, speculated the scientific community, Elvis can be found on other planets.

• *The Big Bang*. The downscaling of our conception of the universe also applied to theories of its creation. Analysis of the found mass yielded data disproving the Big Bang theory and supporting the conclusion that, however bizarre it seems, the universe is in fact the ambitious science project of a five-dimensional high school junior. The "background radiation," it is now thought, is the buzzing of the student's alarm clock as it wakens him for school.

This theory, at once utterly absurd and teasingly plausible, has found both acceptance and rejection among proponents of organized religion. Traditionally uncertain about their relationship to science, they have found their ambivalence deepened still further. On the one hand, it seems, God does indeed exist. On the other hand, He is a nerd.

THE WAY WE LIVE is not so different from what it has always been. We eat, we drink (though only with a permit), we work, we play, we perform microsurgery on ourselves. Sex and money still excite us, though not as much as lawsuits. But one thing many say has changed is our power of recall. We couldn't say—we can't remember! And do we really care? If we don't know whether things used to be better, *now* is always the best of times.

THE WAY WE LIVE

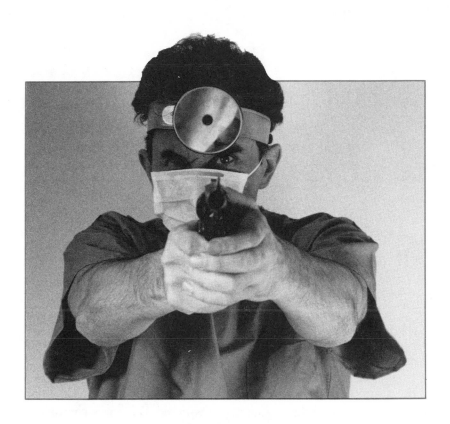

"Your money or your life."
Doctors reduced to earnings of less than $500,000 a year
were forced to demand payment in advance.

CONSUMERS' GUIDE TO DRUGS

THE government deregulated mood-altering and recreational drugs in 1994. Within months the Nader Group had prepared a consumers' guide to today's most popular drugs.

ECSTACY LITE: A milder version of Ecstacy that induces a milder, less embarrassing level of euphoria.

Typical Testimonial: "I suddenly had this contented feeling. Like I'd just been told I had a really good credit rating."

Potential Side Effects: User may experience a very mild depression, equivalent to the sense of loss one feels upon losing a favorite comb.

HEROINETTE: All the side effects of heroin, with none of the mental slowdown.

Typical Testimonial: "Five minutes after shooting up, I was drooling, nodding, and ab-

sentmindedly scratching my arms and legs. Later, I vomited. But I was completely lucid and conscious, so I could enjoy every single second of it."

Potential Side Effects: Loss of friends.

DIRECT ACCESS: An electrode is connected to the neurons in your brain's "pleasure center." An unobtrusive flesh-colored wire runs out of your ear and is connected to a big red button. Each time you push the button, a mild electrical pulse provides a psychoelectrical stimulus directly to a very special part of your brain.

Typical Testimonial: "Like having a five-hour orgasm, with none of the laundry problems."

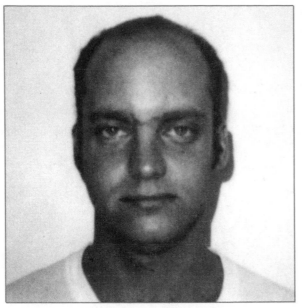

After an unexceptional day at the office or beach, why not unwind with some Ecstacy Lite?
Before...and after. Ah...isn't that just a little bit better?

Potential Side Effects: May make some users ejaculate out of their tear ducts.

ANTICRACK: The perfect antidote to a good hit of crack.

Typical Testimonial: "I'm a crack connoisseur. I can tell good crack from bad crack, and I use both extensively. Anticrack did just as it promised. It took me down to a relaxed, contemplative state, whereby I could calmly and rationally decide to take some more crack. Crack, anticrack, crack, anticrack—I went back and forth like this for quite a while, trying to find an even point. Suddenly a month had passed and I found myself in Milwaukee."

Potential Side Effects: None when used correctly.

EVEN-ODD: Ingesting this pill ensures a fifty-fifty chance that you will die within the next fifteen minutes. Quite a thrill—makes you make the most of the next fifteen minutes. A gambler's delight.

Typical Testimonial: "My whole life passed before my eyes. I swore to myself that if I survived I would spend the rest of my life helping others. I did, and I've dedicated my life to turning other people on to this wonderful drug. At least half of them have reported spiritual awakenings similar to mine."

Potential Side Effects: 50 percent chance of death.

CASH-ON-HAND: You pay a predetermined amount of cash. The dealer then takes you to a secluded location and opens a briefcase full of up to two thousand dollars—in genuine 1980s-style cash money! You are permitted to look at the cash for thirty seconds, or until you faint from excitement. Your cash payment is then added to the dealer's briefcase, making your next Cash-on-Hand high even more profound.

Typical Testimonial: "The second time was even better: seeing my own cash money in there with all that other cash money was just too much. I had to get more cash money so that I could see it again."

Potential Side Effects: May cause irreversible wistfulness and nostalgia for the late 1980s.

WE ARE WHO WE EAT

EATING in the 1990s could be summed up in a single phrase: *Not for cowards*. Haven't we come a long way since we first starting dabbling in hostile foods? Why, I can still remember when sushi was just something you ate to scare your parents if they were visiting from out of town. But look how far we'd advanced by the end of the nineties! When the waiter brought in that live monkey skittering around on the tray, we didn't think twice about stabbing it to death with our chopsticks. . . .

And what about rotten food? Of course America had France to thank for that. It was master chef Jean-Louis Tropgros—and his three-star restaurant Les Deux Magots—who took the credit for introducing *la cuisine pas nouvelle de tout* to an astounded public. Within days, aged food had oozed its way onto our shores and into our hearts. Suddenly ordinary fare seemed so *fibrous* compared to the velvety softness of meals that had been sitting in the sun for a few weeks. We traded in our crisp vegetables for shiny-slick ones, spread our steaks *on* our baked potatoes, and marveled at how much richer pâté seemed when it was coated with thick gray fur. . . .

I, for one, was glad to see the nation's eaters get a little less squeamish as the decade went on. It all ends up in the same place, after all! Still, I couldn't help feeling just a bit worried about all those poor girls with cannibulimia. It's one thing not to squawk when you find a lock of hair in your tuna, but I really have to draw the line at eating other people—don't you? I *know* it was stress-related. I *know* they were just trying to get back at their parents. But really! To see these absolutely lovely little girls, with their manicures and everything, just *huddled up in the corners* at the mall, gnaw-

The Buffalo Wing Chicken, bred with five pairs of wings, was typical of genetically enhanced food.

ing on the leg of some corpse they'd dragged in from the parking lot . . . well, I may be old-fashioned, but it gave me the creeps. And they didn't even bother to use *napkins*.

What *is* it about using food to get back at people, anyway? The nation's farmers decided to punish us city slickers in a *big* way during the past decade. What a bunch of sourpusses! Why, I couldn't count the stalks of asparagus I found with nails hammered into them—the banana skins that had been hollowed out, filled with balled-up Kleenex, and sewn back together again—the apples painted with scary faces. . . . Fellows, why didn't you just lobby Congress to restore price supports instead of being such big sabotage-babies?

Dessert, everyone? That's what the waiters wanted to know, and we caroled a joyful "Oh, what the fuck" in return. In the nineties we all gave in and started bingeing on fat again. Tiresome old skinnies like Jane Brody kept fretting about how suicidal it was, but who cares? I mean, we're all getting older, and the end of the world *is* on its way—right? So what are we worrying about? Shouldn't it be okay to put butter on your Dove Bar if you feel like it? I'd *rather* die any day than go without ice cream on my roast beef—wouldn't you?

The label on the image reads:

GARDEN MACHINERY, CRANE, BLENDER,

Rx: 147876

DIRECTIONS:
Take orally twice a day
with lunch and dinner,
or as directed.

RECOMMENDED DAILY ALLOWANCE:
4-6 ounces

ACTIVE INGREDIENTS:
Ethyl alcohol (ethanol),
organic acids, sulfites,
grape juice.

GRAND VIN

CHATEAU

CH • BAGES

GRAND CRU CLASSÉ

PAUILLAC

MÉDOC

APPELLATION PAUILLAC CON

J. C. CAZES, PropRE

PRECAUTIONS:
Avoid operating a motor
vehicle or heavy machinery
while taking this product.
Do not ingest with red
meat or dessert.

COUNTER-INDICATIONS:
Taking this product during
pregnancy may cause birth
defects. May aggravate
existing renal disorders.
Excessive use may lead to
hepatic dysfunction,
blindness, hallucination,
cardiac arrest and death.
In case of accidental
overdose, induce vomiting.

CONTROLLED PHARMACEUTICAL • SALE OR RE-USE IS PROHIBITED

BY ORDER OF THE SURGEON GENERAL OF THE UNITED STATES

WARNING: TOXIC SUBSTANCE KEEP OUT OF REACH OF CHILDREN

TOASTER, OR ANY OTHER ELECTRONIC

EQUIPMENT WITHIN SEVEN

DAYS OF CONSUMPTION

WILL RESULT IN FINES AND JAIL

SENTENCES

• OPERATION OF A MOTOR VECHICLE, HEAVY MACHINERY, CHAINSAW,

VIN DE SIECLE

What began in the late 1980s as an errant attack on the venerable pleasures of wine, had, by the middle of the 90s, become the focal point of a great national debate. Under sustained pressure from anti-alcohol forces, the Surgeon General moved to curb its "abuse" by limiting the consumption of beer and spirits to odd days in even years and even days in odd ones. Leap years were totally dry.

Yet, faced with mounting epidemiological evidence that moderate wine drinkers lived far longer than total abstainers, the Food & Drug Administration couldn't stop the stomping of grapes. Stuck between the Scylla of neo-Prohibition and the Charybdis of abuse, the Surgeon General had little choice but to declare wine a pharmaceutical. In 1997, wine officially became a drug.

Naturally, this reclassification caused many problems for the hospitality industry. Perhaps the most hard-hit were restaurants. With wine no longer available, except by prescription, many eateries quickly disappeared, unable to compete with hospital commissaries stocked to the rafters with Sancerre and Cabernet. Out-patient clinics began sporting white tablecloths and candlelight service. Emergency rooms installed Cruvinets. Buy-Rite merged with Rite-Aid. Chefs started studying physiology, and nurses oenology.

It wasn't long before illegal wine-bars lined the Mexican and Canadian frontier, offering bottles unregulated by the States. Tijuana has become synonymous with Beaujolais Nouveau, Vancouver with Chianti Classico Riserva. With outlawed cases balanced atop their heads, former pot-smugglers now wade daily across the swift currents of the Rio Grande and into the arms of collectors anxious to keep their cellars from dwindling down to vin de operating table.

MOMMY, DADDY, I'M HOME, I THINK.

AT first nothing seemed different when I got home from school that day. The front door of our condo was kind of hard to open, but that's happened a million times before. Estrella was watching TV, but she's always doing that. She didn't turn around, just kind of chirped out "Hi-honey-cookie-onda-counter" the way she does every day. She's supposed to take care of me after school, but she doesn't speak almost any English. So I took some cookies and went into my bedroom and saw the dog on the bed, and that's when I sort of started to wonder.

I mean, all my stuff was there—my dolls my Nice 'n Nautilus machines and my fridge and stove and everything. (Mom put a kitchenette in my bedroom so that I could get my own breakfast without bothering her and Daddy. They need an hour alone with the newspapers before they leave for their offices.)

It was the dog that looked different. He was a cat. I just *know* we have a dog, not a cat. I've seen Estrella cleaning up after him!

I was going to ask Estrella about the cat when the phone rang. It was Mommy saying she'd be home late again and I should microwave something for dinner. I didn't get a chance to ask her about the cat. And when I got off the phone, Estrella had gone home.

The next couple of weeks were okay but I wondered if something weird was going on. When I saw Mommy and Daddy on weekends, Mommy kept calling Daddy "Ted" instead of "Brad." And Daddy was always on the phone —with his clients. But it's supposed to be *Mommy* who's always on the phone with her *patients*! And a couple of times I caught them looking at me funny. I mean different funny from the way they usually look at me funny. I started to wonder if somehow they weren't my parents. But then I thought, how can that be? All the stuff in the condo looked just the same as always.

Well, we finally figured it out the first Saturday morning in the next month. That's when Mommy and I go to the supermarket. A lady came up to Mommy and said, "Excuse me, but I think you've got my daughter. Is *this* little girl yours?" And she pointed to the girl standing next to her.

So the mommy I was with said, "Well, I'm not sure. What's *your* little girl's name supposed to be?" And the other lady said, "Juliana. She's in fourth grade. No, fifth. No, third." Well, Juliana *is* my name, and I *am* in the third grade. So then I was starting to think that maybe that other lady *was* my mommy. And when I looked in her grocery cart, I knew she was. Because she was buying Fruity Pebbles, and that's my favorite food.

So the mommy I was with invited them home with us to straighten things out. It turned out the school limo driver got our zip code mixed up and dropped me and the other girl in each other's demo-zones. I was so glad to get back home and see my own stuff again, even though it was the same.

It was too bad about the dog, though. It's my job to feed him, but the other girl didn't know that, so he starved to death. Mommy says she'll buy me a new one when she gets a lunch hour.

At least I guess it's Mommy. But I don't think Mommy has any white shoes, and this lady does. It doesn't really matter, though. Estrella can go with me to get the dog. I think it's Estrella.

ADVERTISING:
THE AGONY AND THE ECSTASY

ADVERTISING in the 90s looked for new worlds to conquer, and found them. At the forefront was Whittle Communications, whose pioneering efforts to introduce ads to classroom television in the late 80s led, in 1993, to the creation of "the Classies," a series of awards for excellence in the field of commercials made for classroom television. Its annual prime-time (9:00 A.M. to 3:00 P.M.) awards ceremony, hosted by Bill Cosby™, attracted heavy sponsorship.

Whittle also pioneered so-called "splatter" advertising, a trade term for placing ads on every surface visible to the human eye. Whittle located graphic ads near (or over) elevator floor numbers, audio ads on private answering machines, and video ads on closed-circuit TV security monitors in high-rise apartments and office buildings.

Whittle's domination of splatter advertising encountered only one significant setback. In August of 1996, the company inaugurated its placement of both video-only and audio-video ads on the screens of air traffic controllers. The ads were limited to brief flashes, averaging between .45 and 1.7 seconds. Those at the higher end of the scale created no problems; but the shorter ones (between .45 and .85 sec-onds in duration) were perceived only subliminally.

One tragic day in early September, the entire afternoon shift at the Denver airport traffic control tower stood up and, to a man, drove en masse to a nearby Wendy's. Chaos followed. Nearly 500 died, and twice as many were injured in the ensuing air collisions or, "non-near misses."

Whittle also investigated the potential of the human body. The company contracted with prospective surgery patients to advertise pharmaceuticals and technical equipment directly on their internal organs. The result: pinpoint targeting of the market by the manufacturer, as products for renologists were promoted only on kidneys, those for cardiologists only on hearts, and so forth. A 1997 study showed that fully 86 percent of neurosurgeons questioned reported "significant recognition and recall" of an ad for the Maui Hilton when it appeared sutured to a patient's medulla oblongata.

But, many Americans reasoned, if my spleen can sell BMWs, why can't the rest of me? Thus was born the so-called "nonentity endorsement," the corporate sponsorship of private individuals who, in the course of their daily lives, promoted their underwriter's products or services. Individuals taped every waking moment of their lives, providing documentation of how often they mentioned their sponsor's product, and submitted cassettes along with their invoice for residuals.

In this field, demography was destiny: the kind of sponsor a person attracted depended on how he or she fit the company's product image, how many (and what sort of) friends and business associates he or she had, etc. There were, unavoidably, inequities, and those rejected for sponsorships learned to their dismay that, in the field of nonentity endorsements, "It's not what you know, but who you know, and how many of them." By the end of the decade, sociologists had identified a new lower class: the undersponsored.

Many of this group consisted of rural families who spoke only, and incomprehensibly, to each other. Defying demographers' predictions, however, low-income minorities did well. Many participated in mass endorsements of athletic shoes, as companies such as Puma, Adidas, Nike, etc., sponsored youth gangs and incorporated "wilding." One ad promised high style "both on the court, and in court," while a television spot for Converse simply stated "Converse All-Stars: for all-star cons."

The industry found new markets—and artistic credibility—in the creation of "adver-

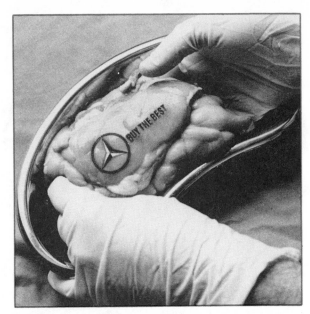

Whittle Communications breakthrough in "internal advertising" on the organs of surgery patients specialized in big-ticket items.

tainment" vehicles: TV shows in which the line between program and ad was obliterated in favor of a seamless, realistic melange of dialogue and ad copy, story line and storyboard. Such shows as "L.A. Lawn" (John Deere), "The Golden Grills" (Kingsford Charcoal Briquettes), "shirtysomething" (Van Heusen) helped pioneer the form. In the Pacino-DeNiro-Hoffman remake of *The Treasure of the Sierra Madre*, fans of the John Huston classic heard an old line take an exciting new twist: "We don' need no steenking bah-dges," sneers Jack Nicholson as the head *bandito*. "We clean them up with Formula 409, *hombre*, and they smell niiiiiiiice . . ."

It has been a decade of the individual: countless individuals advertising to countless other individuals. Indeed, statisticians working for Leo Burnett USA have calculated that, by the year 2010, everyone in America will have been in a commercial. "Put it this way," noted industry innovator Jay Chiat. "In the future, everyone will be famous for fifteen seconds."

SEX ADVANCES IN THE 90s

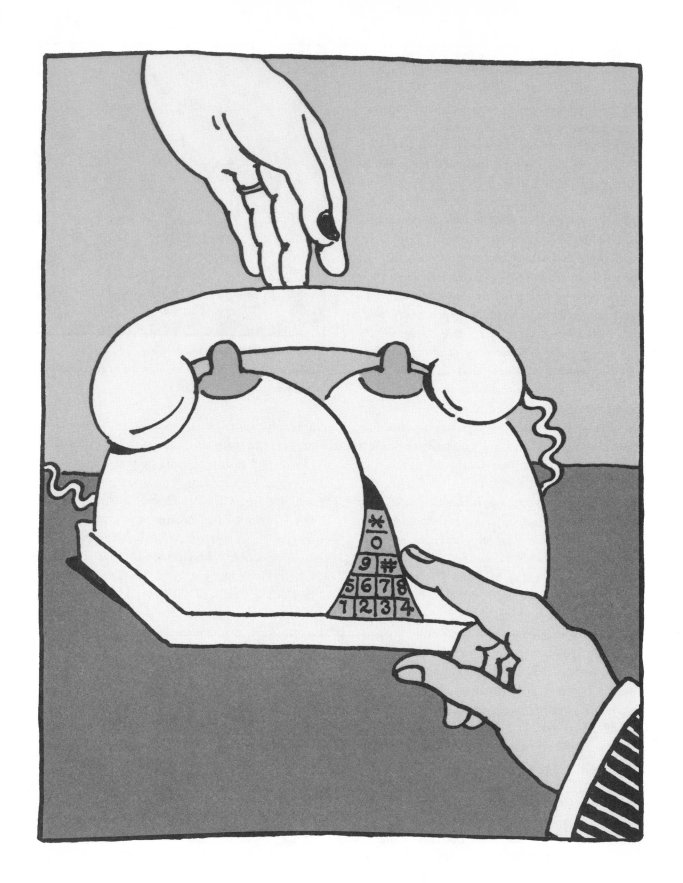

SEX ADVANCES IN THE 90s

SEX IN THE 90's

JIM AND JUDY JURASSIC, 95 AND 92½ RESPECTIVELY, STARS OF THE X-RATED HIT, "BITE MY BYPASS." TOWARD THE END OF THE CENTURY AN AGING AMERICAN POPULATION, STILL AS HORNY AS EVER, BECOMES A RIPE MARKET FOR A WHOLE NEW INDUSTRY: GEEZER-PORN.

SEX IN THE 90'S

Polygamy makes a comeback! Once regarded as the mark of savagery, having multiple spouses is now seen as a logical way to ease the mate shortage and cut the divorce rate. Above: swim-fin magnate Irv Splendid legally weds the lovely Moe sisters, Eeny, Meeny and Marnie.

S.P.I.N.

SPIN (Subscriber Preference Initiated News) began modestly. "Are you an infomaniac?" asked its initial ad campaign in 1992, "or are you looking for action on *your own* terms?"

SPIN had a simple premise. Based on your preference menu it selected news from the more than 800 channels and services available worldwide, and compiled a thirty-minute newscast "just for you." It scanned your reaction (saccadic eye movements, changes in skin temperature, etc.) and further refined the selection for the next newscast. After a week or so, your nightly newscast was a remarkably accurate reflection of your character, background, tastes, and prejudices.

Getting the news they wanted, rather than the news networks decreed they needed, appealed to people. SPIN was an overnight success. Network response was desperate. Singing news gave way to topless news, then to all-nude news and finally to the notorious "snuff" news in which many old-line journalists (amongst them Dan Rather and Jeff Greenfield) lost their lives. SPIN promoters for their part dealt network news a deathblow, when, in 1994, under the rubric of "reenactment" they began effectively creating news to fit subscriber tastes. By the middle of the decade they were routinely shooting wars, disasters, demonstrations, and social upheavals on soundstages, and presenting them as real events. (The widely differing accounts of who had run in, and won, the 1994 election was but one result.)

Critics, some of whom announced the "death" of consensus reality, were answered with the argument that traditional news had always been an inextricable mix of what people imagined or hoped was happening and what was actually happening. SPIN, say its most ardent advocates now, has actually created a superior reality which is measurable, controllable, and predictable. And since no two individuals can possibly agree on what is actually happening in the world, the conflicts and injustices which arise when large numbers of people agree on something are now impossible. (This superior reality has been dubbed the "newsphere.")

On the eve of the millennium, what can be seen on, or retrieved from, the SPIN cycles of more than forty million Americans presents a unique profile of every single individual. An actual record of his or her deepest hopes and fears, a tangible reflection of each identity. With the right access code, we can see, for the first time in history, what the past and present look like through another's eyes.

The question is: do we want to? George Carlin, curator of the Museum of Words in Santa Barbara, takes a New Year's Eve spin through some identities:

TAKANABE 81 70000 Z/Z 23MK

JENNINGS: The 1996 campaign theme of all four Demographic Parties will be "Decline into Semi-Controlled Weirdness of a Type We Can Handle" . . . WIPE/JENNINGS: . . . such chaos that the country has accidentally elected its first black President . . . WIPE/JENNINGS: . . . a lone assassin named merely Buzzy, who evidently managed to place a poisoned Ding Dong on the inaugural breakfast plate of Mr. Diddley. Vice President Zamfir, master of the pan flute, has quietly

assumed power in a ceremony marked by the public flogging of several hundred immigrant invalids from Bermuda. . . .CU ZAMFIR: When I have fun, someone's gotta pay . . . WIPE/JENNINGS: . . . overthrown by a cabal of highly attractive fishermen. The currency has been changed to all dimes. The new coins will carry an abstract drawing of an elderly blowfish, defecating in a cigar box and the motto MY TEETH ARE FINE . . .

JOE K. 44 nw2-7 T/R 500K

. . . bat choirs . . . mandatory hat inspection . . . canned bottles . . . all-static radio . . . involuntary perpetual foreplay . . . doubt shrines . . . surrogate in-laws . . . organ swapping . . . cheese cults . . . the Museum of Cowardice . . .

ROTH 01 80611 T/D 100K

1993 Workweek reduced to Wednesday. Awright! Six-day weekends! Party hard! 1994 Techno-Blast introduces first Party Barn. Awright! Ten square miles. Half a million heads in ONE ROOM! You can get in, but you can't get out. Airborne cocaine, forced amphetamine enemas. Pre-deafened metal groups on steroids. Eight-foot 400-pound lead singers. Ritually slaughtered at end of set. Rabid pit bulls set loose at midnight. PARTY ANIMALS! Awright! Everyone with horn implants and stun knuckles. Fatalities by the thousand. Our barn's badder than your barn. Life in the leather lane. Those were the days, my friend . . .

Z. WARHOL 01 70707 T/A Inher/MK +

CONTINUOUS EXPLOSIONS. DATES 1995, 1996, 1997 SUPER. VOICE-OVER: The Bow Tie People of Chicago burnt the 60-story Tampon Building to the ground by setting fire to the "String," an oak sculpture which adorns Tampon Plaza. . . . The New Jersey Devils won the Stanley Cup by turning the Statue of Liberty 180 degrees to face

Newark. . . . The Even Newer Right has been subdued by the Boss Militia. The postal employees were armed with a new tactical gas weapon which induces unpleasant childhood memories. . . .

LUPI L. 73 sp-1-sp T/? 617K

Aroma thought . . . rectal harmonicas . . . diet gruel . . . random dentistry . . . grief tournaments . . . musical autopsy . . . laser tap dancing . . . all-wool spaghetti . . . cloud ownership animal-generated music . . . tree sex . . .

THOMAS MT 01 10180 T/H 730K

1993 Dance finally advances to level long foreseen by the avant-garde: aimless gyrations performed at home and described to critics over the phone. 1994 Opera reverts to its classical form: random stabbing of the overweight. 1995 Lincoln City Hall presents play directed by Gregory Mosher about a theater curtain that won't open. 1997 Skinheads adopt classical music; concerts indistinguishable from soccer riots. 1998 London Symphony Orchestra converts to all-whistling format. 1999 Courts limit string quartets to one string per player . . .

BETSY LN 01 90048 T/B 221K

1993 Spavin First National Savings and Loan of Oklahoma City repossesses Brazil. 1994 Japan repossesses U.S. 1995 Guam repossesses Japan (loophole in 1945 surrender terms). 1996 Elton John repossesses Guam. 1997 Island Records repossesses Elton John. 1998 Poodle dies. 1999 Nothing much so far . . .

M. QUAYLE 00 000 T/O 00

Second Lady . . . official mourner . . . First Lady . . . official mourner . . . Madam Senator . . . first mourner . . . President Elect . . . Empress of Gaia . . . Armageddon Director . . . Saint Marilyn of Indiana . . . Divine Fiancée . . . Mrs. God the Father . . . official mourner . . .

POVITCH M. 01 NTWRK T/NONE 777MK

9:00 A.M. "Say What?" A deal crack dealer answers audience questions. 9:01 "All My Chancres." Medical/insult fone-in. 10:00 "The Wildings." Topless/bottomless snuff soap with occasional language. 11:00 "Take That!" Slow-motion sequences of foreigners being beaten to death with chains. 1:00 "The Universal Paving Act." (Documentary) Pulped trees force-fed to the homeless. 3:00 "Neo-Gong Show." Mental patients castrate themselves with blunt bread knives, but are gonged anyway.

JOE K. 44 nw2-7 T/R 500K

1993 Spiro Agnew comeback . . . cow racing . . . fiber and grain bars . . . ambition intervention . . . 1994 Radar bow ties . . . small mammal rape . . . weather gambling . . . designer melanomas . . . 1995 Salvation Air Force . . . drive-by pregnancy . . . nude parachuting . . . foreskin vests . . . 1996 . . .

CARLIN G. 01 909 T/T ?MK

WELCOME TO SPIN. HERE IS A SPIN-FLASH: Tonight at nine . . . a ten-man Zen skateboard team goes off a cliff at Big Sur. Plus end-of-the-century special: rare tape of PETER JENNINGS picking through a dumpster looking for pizza crusts.

STAY TUNED.

JUST look at all the new buttons you have on your video remote control: Buy, Sell, UPscale, DOWNscale, Short Programming Attention Span Mode (SPASM) and Colorize. Go ahead—hit your AutoSelect button and see whether your TV decides to show you a high-demo series like "N.Y. M.B.A." or a low-demo one like "Garroting Tonite." And now tell me that we haven't progressed.

Like a fatty who allows himself bursts of gluttony, we finally had to make a deal with advertisers' pandering. It was only fair. For years, advertisers had given us free entertainment and information and we showed our gratitude by zapping their ads, zipping past their programs, and even boycotting their products. America was in the throes of an industry-wide crisis.

The solution came from the country's foremost media factory, GanNet (the offspring of the 1992 mega-merger of Gannet Communications, CBS, MGM, HBJ, KKR, P&G, and the WPP advertising conglomerate). The direct-response whizzes at GanNet found a way to force advertising down our throats and still make us smack our lips and thank them for it. They also made sure that advertisers need never again reach one extraneous consumer.

Thanks to the revolution in video home shopping—which made it possible for us to buy anything through TV, from BMWs to colored condoms—GanNet could force us to paint psychographic self-portraits. After all, they now controlled programming *and* commercials *and* purchasing.

Programs were designed in an ever more modular manner. Scenes became shorter and shorter (to fit shorter and shorter attention spans). Plot and character consistency disappeared. Without us noticing, GanNet could now actually change the content of a program *while it was airing* to suit the demographic we'd revealed by our purchases. Soon you couldn't just turn on your set, suffer through the commercials and sales pitches—even if they suited your demographic—and enjoy your favorite show. The TV wouldn't let you see it until you'd bought the right products and the right number of them; conversely, if you found yourself watching a channel whose demographic was beyond your means, you were assaulted with nothing but commercials pitching offensive but expensive products until you flipped to a channel selling products you could afford. *Your* channel.

GanNet's guiding principle was simple: We are what we buy. Few would now prefer the hit-and-miss marketing methods of the eighties, but some objections have been raised that GanNet—which controls some 85 percent of all purchases in the United States—has stratified the nation through its "Purchasing Is Destiny" policies. GanNet CEO, sprightly thirty-eight-year-old Merv Griffin, defended his company against this charge on a recent episode of the Rev. Oprah Winfrey's "Sexual Perversity in Chicago" news program. "A demographic society was the dream of the Founding Fathers," he declared. "We've made that a reality. If you don't like the demo you're in, you can buy your way out. Right, Oprah?"

TORTS 'N COURTS

RICHARD Marbury awoke one June morning at 6:00 A.M. to the roar of his neighbor, William Madison, mowing the lawn around Madison's tennis court. Marbury did what any upper-middle-class homeowner of the 90s would do—he buzzed a button next to his bed, and his family lawyer stepped into Marbury's room.

Marbury's lawyer walked next door with an order requiring Madison to cease and desist. Madison refused. Madison's family lawyer appeared and took over the case. Suit was filed twenty minutes later at the corner legal mall.

Marbury vs. Madison was typical of the millions of cases filed as law pervaded society and the trend toward "family lawyers"—one or more lawyers who lived with a family and tended to its day-to-day legal needs—created more, if lower-paying, job opportunities. The family lawyer might negotiate a husband out of a traffic ticket, bring suit against the A & P for a spoiled quart of milk, write a legal contract for Chinese takeout, or settle a damage suit involving the son's skateboard. It was all in a day's work.

Courts became busier than ever as these and other new torts were recognized:

• In Orlando, Florida, a group of partygoers successfully filed a class action against a would-be storyteller who "led plaintiffs down the path of a long and involved joke, and then did forget the punchline."

• In Waxahachie, Texas, three diners, the local restaurant critic, a sommelier, the chef, and the owner of the Vin du Extraordinaire Restaurant were all found to have independent standing to sue a hapless customer who loudly ordered the 1962 Chateau Talbot (a Saint-Julien) to accompany a dish of *Allumettes à l'andalouse.*

• In Seattle, Washington, a woman was granted a divorce on the grounds that her husband "cruelly refused, on countless occasions, to ask directions while the couple did drive along the back roads of King County." The court reasoned that such an obstinate refusal to conduct oneself in a normal human fashion was clearly a form of mental abuse.

While the business of courts grew, the right to

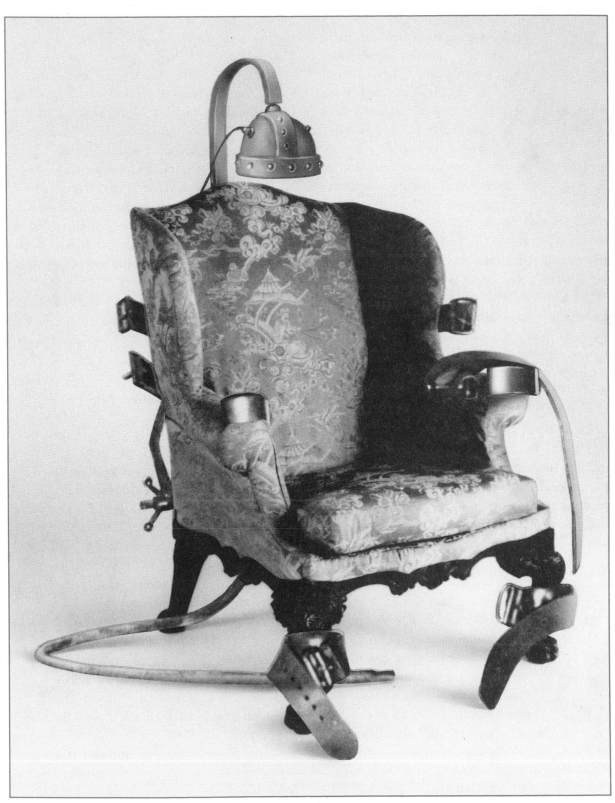

A "kinder, gentler" execution was assured to Death Row inmates with the introduction
of the low-voltage electric chair. Just sit back, ease into the copper slippers and say goodbye.

a jury trial remained. The difficulty of finding jurors was immense. The result was the creation of a professional class of jurors. They followed a "circuit," traveling from town to town and court to court, often rendering dozens of verdicts a day. Even with the advent of professional jurors, the court systems nevertheless became so overburdened that private enterprise stepped in. A common feature on the American landscape by the end of the 1990s was the "mom-and-pop legal store" (in larger suburban areas, the "legal mall" or "Mall of Justice" performed the same function). Mom-and-pop legal stores were all-in-one systems where litigants could purchase, under one roof, a grand jury probe, indictment, pretrial proceedings, trial (with or without jury), sentencing, appeals, incarceration and/or execution, and parole.

Legal ethics panels eagerly found that nothing in the Code of Professional Responsibility militated against such enterprises. Quite the contrary - the concept was found to be "on all fours" with a lawyer's duty to "proceed with the orderly and economical course of justice."

Not surprisingly, the most controversial result of such deregulated justice was its use of the death sentence. Requests for change of venue in capital cases were usually honored by moving the hearing from the front to the back of the store, or out into the parking lot. Automatic appeals and requests for stays of execution were heard on the spot and always denied. Methods of execution also varied widely. Thanks to climatic changes in Florida, prisoners were often just left out in the sun. (As the saying went: "It was so hot, we fried a guy on the sidewalk.") By contrast, in Philadelphia on Christmas Eve 1996, 158 prisoners were electrocuted simultaneously on top of City Hall. When lit they spelled out MERRY CHRISTMAS—JOYOUS NOEL. Much had changed since President Bush's call for a "kinder, gentler nation" and the widespread introduction in the early 90s of the low-voltage electric chair.

Finally, even as some lawyers became, in effect, household retainers, others became household names. In August 1993, New York's Baychaleefe and Katz made its first major league trade: three arbitrage specialists and a real estate permanent associate for a black woman lawyer who was at the top of her class at the University of Texas.

"This kid's got everything," said a B & K scout of Coretta Abernathy. "We'd never waste her on the actual practice of law. She can do it all: show up at law schools, talk to the legal press, pose for partnership pictures. She gives us real strength in the area where we need it most."

In May 1997, the trade of the decade was made by lawyers' agent Norby Lexis: two Yale law journal editors each signed a three-year, $7.4-million contract with Los Angeles' Bau, Down & Creigh. Bonuses were built in for successful oral arguments and briefs in excess of 150 per season.

At the end of the decade, lawyers' "stats" roll off the tongue of every kid in America. They know the guy in Montana with the best IJP (Impassioned Juror Plea) in the Western League, they pack the courtrooms of New York to watch the guys with the best PBP (Plea Bargain Pitch).

Some say this massive popularization and democratization of the law has made justice a joke. Tell that to a kid at Yale Pre-Law School. He'll slap you with a kindergarten-class action suit that'll knock your socks off.

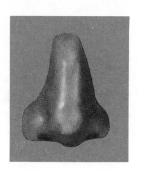

MEDICINE: YOUR MONEY OR YOUR LIFE

THE nineties were marked by medical breakthroughs so miraculous that we may never recover from them.

True, science did find cures for the great killer diseases that had caused human misery from time immemorial. Cancer, heart attacks, pneumonia, and even AIDS were all conquered.

Unfortunately, they were replaced by new, greater killer diseases. Schnurm syndrome, runny nose fever, and pedigiantosis (a grotesque swelling of the feet, sometimes to boxcar size) wiped out millions. Exploding brain disease made leaving home a hazardous and often revolting experience.

Though the Pentagon denied it, some thought the new ailments were related to an accidental fire that burned down the Army's top-secret Lt. William Calley Laboratory in Baton Rouge, Louisiana, thereby unleashing on the populace more than 3,500-exciting, creative new viruses designed for biological warfare.

By 1992, rising medical costs had driven most of the nation's insurance companies into bankruptcy, greatly changing the doctor-patient relationship. Cash registers and meters became common sights in medical offices and operating rooms.

In 1994, the Supreme Court decided by a 5–4 vote that a physician in Galveston, Texas, could not be sued for malpractice by the widow of an assault victim who had needed fourteen stitches to close a knife wound but at $150 a stitch could only afford three, plus a Band-Aid.

Hospitals in New England required patients without Gold Cards to leave an organ on deposit before they could be admitted to surgery.

In many cities, when critically sick people were connected to artificial life-support systems, these in turn were connected via computerized telephone lines to the patient's bank, ensuring that his bill could be paid. If the patient's account ran dry, the bank sent an electronic disconnect signal, causing the patient to be automatically unplugged.

The procedure could be stopped only if the patient received a cash transfusion from a bank loan officer or, in New Jersey, from a certified Mafia loan shark.

In mid-decade, the better hospitals began bearing a remarkable resemblance to private clubs. Wealthy people of high social rank found it easiest to join, but all applicants had to be voted in by a majority of patients. Trying to impress the entrance committee, more and more people donated money to their favorite hospitals even before they became sick. The competition became so intense that a Florida real estate developer, who had given $250,000 to the Pompano Beach Medical Center, asked to see his wing and was shown to the Gerard J. Pincus Memorial Tongue Depressor.

Incredibly, doctors became even more arrogant. Many now refused to make office calls. Patients had to travel to golf courses for treatment.

Hospitals in poorer neighborhoods tended to be dilapidated and jammed with drug dealers who had been wounded by rivals. By 1996, for the sake of efficiency, most of these were merged with prisons. Checking into an emergency room now constituted a legal admission of guilt. Patients were read their rights before treatment, then taken to the operating cell or, in difficult cases, the electric gurney.

These hospitals were staffed primarily by Pakistanis, Bangladeshis, and a large influx of New Guineans, who effected some miraculous cures but had a tendency to eat the recently deceased.

The shortage of qualified doctors eventually gave rise to the popular and affordable MedArcade system, a network of completely automatic coin-operated medical treatment and diagnostic centers.

All types of treatment were offered, even complex surgical procedures. In most cases, a patient could feed eight or ten quarters into the slot, load himself into one of the twenty surgical chambers, and be out in five minutes, not only healthier but washed and spin-dried as well.

Though the robodocs, with their advanced laser surgery technology, were highly reliable, patients could not afford to be careless in positioning themselves on the operating table; occasionally one in need of an appendectomy would have his nose removed.

Many MedArcades were located in shopping malls and became popular "hangout" spots for local youth. The most interesting operations invariably drew a spirited crowd of kibitzers watching through the little window and betting on whether or not the patient would survive.

Somewhat more expensive were home robotic surgery kits. In the late 90s, these became a national craze. But in 1999, Congress passed a bill restricting their use after a nine-year-old California boy successfully transplanted the head of a Labrador retriever onto the body of his six-year-old sister. And vice versa.

The other major medical trend of the decade followed from the discovery of cures for cancer and heart disease. Many people who had died of these illnesses and been cryogenically preserved were brought back to life. Unfortunately, there was as yet no cure for freezer burn. The result was a glut of old but very healthy people who looked like bad frozen hamburger.

The medical waste problem on New Jersey's beaches worsened in the nineties.

D.I.S.T.R.A.C.T.

1992 was the year in which the average adult's attention span, after years of slow decline, plunged dramatically to 25.4 seconds.

The first signs of accute D.I.S.T.R.A.C.T. (discontinuous trajectory of cortical thought) were shrugged off by officials as part of the downward curve in attention span that seemed to correlate with the premiere of "Bonanza" in September 1959.

As one bizarre incident followed another, they would soon acknowledge the serious threat posed by D.I.S.T.R.A.C.T. to our social organization.

In 1993, at Cape Reagan, Florida, the maiden flight of Akai's *Yojimbo* transport shuttle was snafued when operations commander Lee Alzalter stopped counting down at "four" and asked a coworker if he knew where he could find a colorized version of *Four Faces West* with Joel McCrae. Confused computer sensors immediately destroyed the massive spacecraft along with its cargo of string bound for Spacelab. Said Alzalter at the inquest, "One thought just led to another." In 1994, at Princetown, Minnesota, medical malpractice suits soared as surgeons routinely digressed from standard procedure in the OR. A patient at the Dick Clark Clinic charged that renowned specialist Dr. Rufus Bowler had sutured a valuable new kidney onto the palm of his left hand. Bowler pleaded D.I.S.T.R.A.C.T., explaining that he had been thinking ahead to that evening's deciding Cubs-Indians World Series game.

Public abandonment escalated as couples unintentionally marooned their partners in cafés, banks, and movie theaters. "She just forgot she came in with me " ran the typical complaint. "She walked out of the ladies' room, went over to the bar, picked up a high school kid, and split. The waiter never brought my food, either. I was so depressed when I left the place I took one of the cute little terriers tied up outside. I didn't have him when I got home, though. I think I left him in the elevator."

A May 1997 White House statement insisted there was no "so-called D.I.S.T.R.A.C.T. problem on Pennsylvania

Avenue" and that "executive business or whatever is proceeding normally, unaffected by . . . the fact . . . that the attorney general was definitely not in the Miami hotel room when the alleged 'boogie shower' took place."

D.I.S.T.R.A.C.T. therapists eventually began organizing the population into discrete buddy groups known as support spansules. Essentially, members of a support spansule pool their attention spans to function in a normal manner. Each spansule of twenty persons is thus a car pool, a work squad, a dining club, viewing group, etc. For instance, when an executive loses interest during a business call, a SpanPal jumps in and continues the conversation from the break-point. And a twenty-man spansule—with intense effort and using their attention spans in rotation—can usually get through a one-hour public performance. As a fail-safe backup, each member is equipped with an E-belt, in effect an electrified corset, which zaps its owner every twenty or thirty seconds. (Wide and varied abuses of the E-belt have been reported.)

A spansulized society is necessitating changes in the architecture of the workplace. In order to accommodate, say, the flight crew of a jetliner, grouped in spansules of twenty pilots, twenty navigators, and so on, planes are now designed with enormous cockpits, bulging out of the nose. With office space at a premium, an era of gigantism began. Restaurants require space for small armies of cooks, waiters, and maître d's, not to mention a score of lounge pianists. In the theatre a cast of thousands has become the rule just to ensure the continuity of the dialogue.

Written by Donald Fagen, with the members of SP. 3 7005 150, Montclair, N.J.

Essentially, members of a support spansule pool their attention spans to function in a normal manner.

SPORTS go on forever. Wherever two or more fans gather together, two or more athletes will smash each other's faces in for money, until one cries "Uncle." In an uncertain world it's comforting to know that these principles are for keeps: blood on the ice is good, but brains are better. Betting is a sport like any other. Underdogs deserve to lose. Play ball!

DOES A BEAR BOX IN THE WOODS?

THE GREEKS HAD A GAME FOR IT

THE BARCELONA OLYMPICS AT A GLANCE

ARMS FROM THE MIDDLE EAST

SPORTS

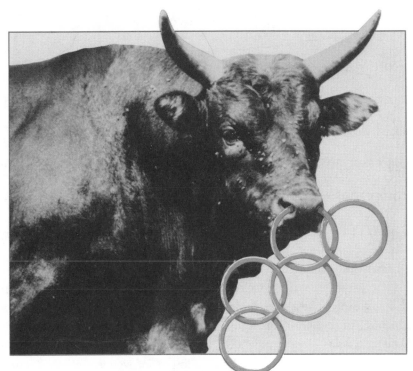

Ferdinand the Bull in a new role:
champion of the 1992 Barcelona Olympics.

DOES A BEAR BOX IN THE WOODS?

BY 1997, Iron Mike Tyson's record stood at 161 wins, no losses, 147 by KO, and forty of those in the first two rounds. But his purses had dwindled to a few hundred thousand dollars per fight.

Desperate to attract an audience, any audience, manager Don King resorted to circus-style promotions—namely the "Chess Championship," in which Tyson

fought three contenders at the same time, with one hand literally tied behind his back. Whether it was because all three opponents were real chess masters, with Coke-bottle glasses and a combined chest expansion of seventy-three inches, or because the fight took place in Minsk, Russia, the audience stayed away in droves. It appeared as if the heavyweight championship would simply disappear through lack of contenders.

But in the spring of 1997, promoter Bob Arum, who had mined the Leonard vs. Duran, Leonard vs. Hearns, Hearns vs. Duran, Duran vs. Leonard, Leonard vs. Hearns, Hearns vs. Duran roundabout into the old age home, announced he was entering the heavyweight arena with a 500-pound challenger called Snuffy, a female Alaskan brown bear.

The challenge was accepted and the date set for that summer. King wanted the fight to be held in Las Vegas, while Arum leaned toward the cooler climes of Montana. Arum also demanded a small ring with a tree stump in the middle, while King insisted that marksmen be placed at each corner of the ring armed with 12-gauge shotguns in case Snuffy forgot the rules.

Splitting the estimated one hundred million dollars proved equally difficult. King wanted forty million for Tyson, forty million for himself, and the rest Arum and Snuffy could divide any way they liked. Arum was outraged. He wanted nothing for himself, forty million for Snuffy, and another twenty million for the Animo-American Fresh-Air Fund.

By the time the purse was finally sorted out, the fight had to be postponed. Snuffy had gone into hibernation. The match was rescheduled for the summer of 1998.

By April both contestants were once again in training. Tyson revealed to reporters that he

TALE OF THE TAPE:

SNUFFY:

Height:	8'8"
Reach:	71"
Weight:	514 lbs.
Chest:	(Unexpanded) 64"
Chest:	(Expanded) Unknown
Waist:	13'6"
Bicep:	Anyone's guess

had dismissed his sparring partners and was working out with a tree stump.

Arum boasted that Snuffy hadn't dismissed her sparring partners; she had never been able to get any in the first place. Through her interpreters, Snuffy added that not only was she going to kick Tyson's ass, but she was going to eat it, too.

On the big night both fighters started cautiously, trying to spot the other's weakness. Snuffy seemed distracted and ill at ease. Several times she dropped to all fours and smelled Tyson's tracks as if to reassure herself she was fighting the right quarry. Finally Tyson charged Snuffy as she was straightening up and delivered a flurry of punches to her head. His right glove wedged between her jaws. She returned overhand crosses with both right and left paws. But Tyson pulled himself free and retreated to his corner, virtually on top of a marksman who was squinting down the barrel of his gun. Mercifully the bell sounded to end the round.

Between rounds, Tyson explained that he couldn't get in close enough to do any damage because Snuffy's breath was unbearable. And Snuffy's earlier discomfort became clear. No sooner had she reached her corner than she defecated into her trainer's water buckets, filling them both several times.

Some forty pounds lighter, Snuffy came out raring to go. She charged at Tyson and landed two well-timed uppercuts. Tyson covered but he was in trouble. Snuffy could have easily finished him off but suddenly stopped and raised her nose, sniffing the air. Tyson gingerly extended his left arm and dangled it enticingly in front of her. Cornerman Gus Schwarz had coated his gloves with honey. Smelling it, Snuffy leaned in with her chin wide open. A thundering right cross from the champ, followed by a left hook, were all that was needed. The champ had retained his title.

THE GREEKS HAD A GAME FOR IT

4.7 seconds remains the mark to beat for the 100 meters at the Millympic Games to be held over Beijing next summer. Time was when twice that would have been world-class, but the nineties have seen some astonishing breakthroughs in track and field.

Whether sports in space will provide still more surprises in times and lengths remains to be seen: an orbiting stadium, however carefully engineered it may be to re-create on-planet conditions, seems bound to usher in a new era of performance. Fierce jockeying for control of the gravitational field equipment has already racked the Olympic committee. Corporate sponsor McDonald Trump Inc. insists that its 100,000-seat stadium, the Gastrodome, includes state-of-the-art security which will make tampering impossible, but suspicion remains high among the poorer nations (who tend to excel in leaping over obstacles and throwing large objects) that the gravitational force will somehow increase when their athletes are clearing the bar or letting loose the javelin.

In any event, the records of '92 and '96 will be hard to beat. The historic 100-meter time —set by Ibn Ben Hijaz of Lebanon at Barcelona in '92—was actually equaled by Florence Joyner-Kersee in her astounding 200-meter run at the same Olympics. Kersee passed the 100-meter mark at 4.7001, and finished the 200 in 9.55 seconds. She then went on to smash— quite literally— the 400-meter and 800-meter records (21.72 seconds and 45.01 seconds respectively) in the same run. The presence of a 1200-pound bull a few feet behind her (see following pages) was considered unremarkable in Barcelona, where bulls, symbols of an ascendant and new-

ly vigorous Spain, were allowed free rein of the Olympic stadium.

Many current record-holders objected strenuously to the marks set in track and field at Barcelona. (Every track event saw new times, as did many swimming and diving events; broad and high jumps also saw staggering records.) Olympic officials eventually ruled that "bull-assisted" records were valid provided they didn't involve actual contact with the bull (rather to the contrary—avoiding contact with it at all costs), since runners were at least still moving under their own steam. Where actual contact broke records (e.g., in the high jump, when Olaf Borg of Norway was "bull-assisted" over the bar to a height of 18' 7"), the records were ruled invalid.

The broad-jump record set in Barcelona (57' 0" by Mbao Ngutami of Malawi) was in any case surpassed by the 3,427' 5" mark set four years later in Teheran. Teheran had won the prize of hosting the '96 Olympics over massive opposition from other nations, citing its "kinder, gentler Iran" campaign of the early nineties in support of its claim as a fair and impartial host. Nonetheless once athletes were inside the Olympic complex, they found Iranian concepts of sporting behavior decidedly foreign. The broad jump mentioned above, for example, was officially named the Very Long Jump Indeed, and was held on (or extremely near) a precipice named the Cliff of Infidels. The Teheran record, in fact – also Borg's – broke down as 27' 5" horizontally, and 3,400 feet vertically.

The Iranians also transformed the very concept of the high jump. Claiming (with some justification) that no one had ever clarified whether the event meant jumping *up* from the ground, or jumping *down* from a height, athletes found themselves being prodded out of hovering helicopters. The winner, an Iranian ex-paratrooper named only Martyr 40505, survived an impressive fall of 58 feet. Other surprises included the writers' 100-yard dash, won by guest of honor Salman Rushdie in 7.7 seconds (tank-assisted), and the demonstration sport introduced by Iran (its prerogative as host)—the 10-meter stoning.

Once the orbiting stadium is built, Olympic athletes—and their records will be out of this world.

THE BARCELONA OLYMPICS AT A GLANCE

ARMS FROM THE MIDDLE EAST

ANYONE who has not noticed the proliferation of Palestinians on major league pitching staffs has been living in a cave. Over sixty percent of the pitching rosters are made up of young Arabs recruited from the occupied zones for their great throwing arms. Hapim al-Tayyi of the Cincinnati Reds, Kut al-Kalub of the Chicago Cubs, Abu Kir of the New York Yankees, and Abd "Big Sam" al-Samad of the Detroit Tigers dominated the All-Star game proceedings this

year. Between them they only allowed one hit. Astonished fans and a nationwide television audience looked on as Abu Kir, who was on the mound at the time, became so outraged at Darryl Strawberry's line-drive single that he scaled his glove across the infield and hit the Mets star on the thigh as he was legging it up the first-base line. "Their marksmanship is extraordinary," commented Tommy Lasorda, the National League manager.

Authorities have likened the Palestinians' success to the dominance of the Taiwanese in Little League baseball. Increasingly, major league scouts are sent to comb the back alleys of the Gaza and the West Bank to search for first-rate rock throwers. "We look for guys who can throw a rock through the gunport of a weapons carrier at a hundred paces," says Francis Thorpe, a Cleveland Indian scout. "Then we try to sign him up before the Israeli patrols get him. You have to catch these guys on the fly."

Many of the scouts wear native garb to get closer to the action, some even disguised as Arab women, peeking out of the slits above their veils. "The chances of being plugged by a rubber bullet if you're a woman are slightly less," explains Jonathan Dee, a scout for the Chicago White Sox. He says that the only disadvantage for some of the older and more grizzled scouts is that it's difficult to chew and spit tobacco wearing the traditional *chador*.

Around the leagues the Palestinians have become renowned for the whiplash speed of their pitches, a tendency to yell *"Allah akbar!"* ("God is great") as they release the ball, and their unerring accuracy. Giving up a base on balls seems almost a dereliction of duty. Earlier this year Zu l-kara'a, one of six Palestinians on the staff of the San Francisco Giants, walked off the mound rather than give up an intentional walk. The Giants manager, Billy Martin, had to bring in James "Jumbo" Jones to carry out his tactical move.

The Palestinians themselves shrug off their ability to nip the corners of the plate. Says Abd al-Malik, one of the four Palestinians

Hapim al-Tayyi had only one pitch—a fastball he called "The Tankstopper." At 110 m.p.h. it was all he needed.

pitching for the Boston Red Sox, *"El ashal an bashuka besbol al bahr min darb lel Israeli,"* which loosely translated means, "It is easier to hit a catcher's mitt than an Israeli soldier."

The Palestinian dominance has made it tough on young American pitchers aspiring to make it in the big leagues. A Palestinian invariably gets the attention of the pitching coaches. An Arab name is almost an automatic ticket to spring training camp. "The American kids dye their hair black. They'd arrive on a camel if they could," Fred Zinkle of the San Diego Padres coaching staff reports. He laughs. "A farm-belt hayseed walks into camp, the cornstalks just about sprouting from his ears, and you say, 'What's your name, son?' He clears his throat and replies: 'Al-Ra'ad al Kasif.'"

The somewhat relieved beneficiaries of the Palestinians' extraordinary success in the majors have been the Israeli patrols. "Thank God for the big league scouts from the U.S.A.!" is an oft-expressed sentiment. "They've signed the best arms off the street," an Israeli soldier said recently. "The patrols are no longer so hazardous. Some of the guys we run into out there can't hit the broad side of a barn!"

KIDS! In the early 90s the debate raged. Were they an indulgence? Were they pollution? Were they sacred? Disposable? Exchangeable? Some people had none. Some had too many. When it came to kids there was no sense of values. Now, thanks to enlightened government intervention, a comprehensive price structure for new and previously parented children has been established by law. No one ever need wonder again whether their kids are worth it. They are—just look in the Blue Book.

SKINBOARDING

AT HOME WITH BOB SAGET IN THE YEAR 2000

ROE V. WADE

KIDS ON THE BLOCK

THROW ONE FOR THE GIPPER

TELEDUCATION

KEITH HARING'S PICTIONARY

THE WOODSTOCK BABY

KIDS

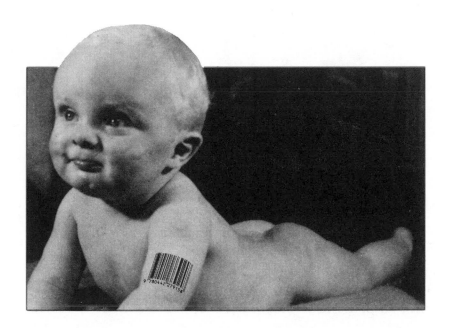

The IICC (Interstate Infant Commerce Commission)
requires that all neo-nates traded in the United States bear the appropriate code.

The 1993
Supreme Court
decision
affirming the
right to sell
advertising
space on or in
the body caused
an explosion in
what soon
became
colloquially
known as
"skinboarding."

SKIN-BOARDING

THE idea was not new; tattoos had existed for centuries. But the use of different frequencies in the microwave spectrum to selectively disrupt the dermis and permanently imprint full-color images on human flesh made the corner-store stylus-artist seem positively medieval.

Brown and Williamson Tobacco was the first to see the commercial possibilities. They offered $2,000 cash plus free day-care services to any parent that would have a newborn child imprinted on the forehead with the "Kool" logo. Income-impaired families immediately took up the offer and the ranks of "Kool Kids" grew rapidly. The 1993 Supreme Court decision affirming the right to sell advertising space on or in the body caused an explosion in what soon became colloquially known as "skinboarding."

Within two years, 34 percent of all income-impaired newborns had commercial affiliations. Skinboarded kids had not only a material edge (financial aid in many cases, fu-

ture job security in others) but a social one too. Branded children had a sense of belonging to a larger family (invaluable in a society where the average marriage lasted eight weeks).

But what began as a privilege rapidly became regarded as a right. Those who'd been branded demanded a greater say in who else received sponsorship. More insidiously, skinboarders developed snobberies about their affiliations. (Vuitton kids, for example, didn't want "just anyone" getting the distinguished logo.) Companies became more selective —or, as some said, discriminatory.

Those who failed to attract sponsorship demanded it as a matter of law—a right the Supreme Court specifically denied them just before leaving on its triumphant 1995 world tour as the opening act for George Michael.

In a celebrated documentary, "The Social Effects of Skinboarding" (1997), one average American mother-to-be—a Mrs. Vera Beltok—gave eloquent testimony to the conflicts she felt about the system:

Mrs. Beltok, this is your first child. What companies have you heard from?

The nice people at Ben and Jerry's. They will help with training—if my baby takes up food-marketing services. We get discounts. We get catering for every birthday till age fourteen. Then there was G.E., AT&T, and Beatrice—they don't pay for the operation, you know, but there is the day-care, the camp, the school, the college, the life-style counseling afterwards. They aren't so friendly but I must be realistic.

How do you feel at twenty weeks?

All the time I worry. Will my baby be born wrong, with two foreheads? How can I tell now that they know ultrasound causes cancer? I hate them all! I will not have my baby marked. I know there will be a social stigma. The other kids will make fun of him for having no skinboard. But what about his freedom? What if I went with Touchstone Films and my baby grew up to hate "buddy" movies?

With the big day almost here, have you resolved the issue of your child's future?

I have. I found a pediatrician. He said the health of my child is more important than commercial interests. So I have made my choice. My baby will skinboard the mark of the American Medical Association. Lifetime discounts on drugs, surgery, liposuction. And that beautiful logo—the snakes and little wings—I'm so proud: my son—the doctor's ad!

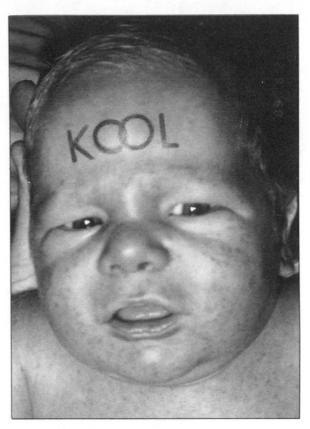

Upward Mobility 90s style: children of income-impaired families could better their lot dramatically by selling space on their bodies to corporate sponsors.

At Home with Bob Saget in the Year 2000

I like to think of myself as an incredibly hip dad, but it's hard to feel like a cool guy when your milk has just started to come in. I can't wear tank tops at the gym and any fabric but 100 percent cotton rubs my nipples raw. Ten years ago I was content just to go to work and let my wife be "Mrs. Homemaker," but now, dammit, I'm proud to be among the growing number of involved dads who love playing an active role in their child's feeding.

When my three kids were young, I'd sometimes look at my wife with envy—"What's it like to be as close with the baby as she is?" "If I could only breast-feed for a moment or two, would my daughter love me more?"

Who knew that science would advance this much in so short a time? My middle girl, now ten, has a baby of her own. Our third daughter, seven, is going steady with a much older man. I gotta admit, it upset my wife and me at first, but what the hell, the guy's not all bad and his son's a bigwig at Toys R Us.

Even today, ten years old seems a bit young to have a baby. But my own flesh and blood created this smaller version of herself knowing full well I was proud to be the maternal force willing to raise the little sucker.

This morning she dumped the baby into my arms and left for work. She's got a job at the Night Court Satellite Channel—all "Night Court" reruns, twenty-four hours a day. She works the phone, taking episode requests from viewers.

My oldest just turned thirteen. Last year we were going to buy her a car as a college graduation present, but all she wanted was that new Harley. I was against her riding such a fast bike, but she rides a motorcycle at work anyway. She's a highway patrolwoman.

So, as I'm writing this, I've got my grandson on my arm and some honey muffins in the solar oven. The problem with a solar-powered oven is that here in Los Angeles there's been no sunlight for seven months. My muffins may never rise.

My daughter's nine-month-old toddler is so damned cute. The boy my wife and I never had. He's already in secretarial school. You see, he's gifted. In fact, we had to register him for the school immediately after my daughter conceived him. So many boys want to be executive assistants these days.

My wife's at work. She returned to law after a decade's hiatus and passed her judicial competency test through the mail. She is now one of the most influential judges in the San Fer-

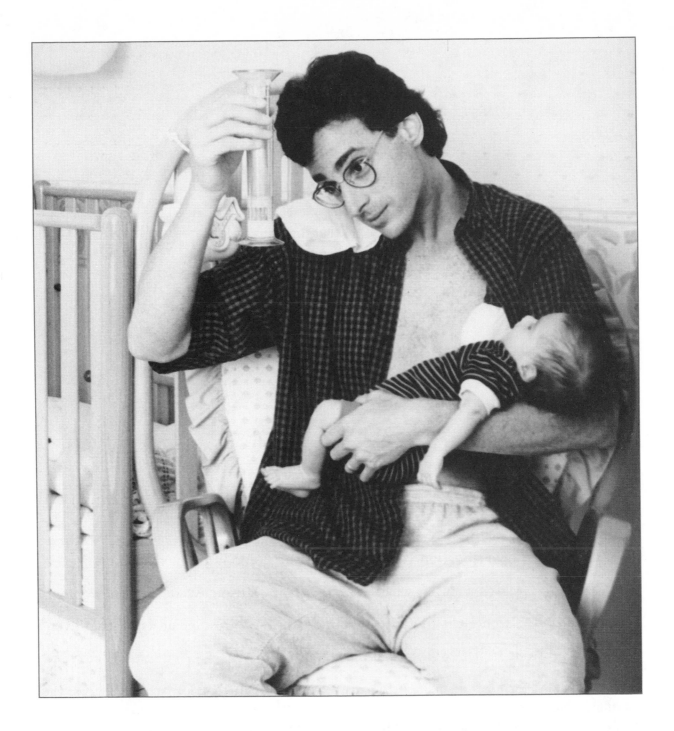

nando Valley. Some of my friends think I should check out this "alleged federal judge job," because my wife works mainly at night, but hell, it's been four years now and geez, she's got six black robes in her closet.

To think I once had a job of my own. In television yet . . .

All through the nineties my agent kept tell-ing me, "There's more to life than show busi-ness." At first I thought she said it so I'd stop asking her for work in show business, but I think subconsciously she had a point. Now I love my life the way it is. I just want to breast-feed my ten-year-old's baby in the warmth and sanity of a peaceful, loving home. Gosh, my nipples are sore.

After forty-three contradictory rulings on abortion in state courts, the court ordered in late 1994 that the long-disputed legal case, Roe vs. Wade, be settled in the public arena.

ROE V. WADE

THE battle over abortion came to a thrilling, bloody climax on New Year's Eve 1994 at Caesar's Palace, when boxing giant Wilson Wade and newcomer Leon "Shad" Roe went at it in a fifteen-round slugfest to resolve an issue that even the U.S. Supreme Court couldn't handle.

Wade, the 287-pound defending champ wearing white-flesh trunks, represented the Right-to-Life movement, while his challenger, Roe, a little-known Texas scrapper weighing in at 263 pounds, wore blood-red trunks and his good-luck pair of high-top Barbara Jordans.

"This is going to be the battle of the century," Roe's promoter/manager, Harvard professor Alan Dershowitz, wearing crimson trunks, told reporters, wearing ink-stained trunks, at ringside. As Wade entered the arena, his only comment to reporters was the reiteration of a personal credo, "Fetus, don't fail me now."

Judging the night's competition were the nine men and women whose indecision led to the fight itself—the nation's highest judicial body, wearing yellow trunks. After forty-three contradictory rulings on abortion in state courts, the court ordered in late 1994 that the long-disputed legal case, Roe vs. Wade, be settled in the public arena, and expressed a strong preference for one with plush leather seats.

Oddsmakers put 3–1 odds on a 5–4 decision, 2–3 odds on a 6–3, 8–1 odds on a 7–2, and 14–1 odds on whether Justice Byron "Whizzer" White would make a pass at Drew Barrymore at the pre-fight mixer.

Judge Sandra Day O'Connor was selected to officiate at the traditional handshake prior to the start of the fight. This event was marred somewhat by some last-minute legal maneuvering by Wilson Wade, who offered O'Connor a bribe to get him a pardon for a 7–11 heist he'd committed earlier in the week.

Observers noticed, as the fight began, that while Roe had the edge in grace and style, there was no disputing Wade's sheer power. Wade kept pummeling Roe's gut while whispering epithets in his opponent's ear about killing innocent children. For the first few minutes it appeared the Right-to-Life forces would take this one in a knockout.

But suddenly, in the fight's second round, Wade began to feel sleepy, with sudden attacks of nausea. Doctors suggested the fight be stopped briefly so that he could have a piece of dry toast. Wade, however, preferred dill pickles and Chunky Monkey ice cream, which he devoured voraciously between rounds. By the seventh round, he'd regained his strength.

Nothing could have possibly foreshadowed the knockout blow, though—a ninth-round killer punch that drew copious blood from Roe's battered face. "A bleeding liberal, a f———ing bleeding liberal!" Wade shouted into Howard Cosell's microphone as reporters crowded around.

Chief Justice Rehnquist, after checking with his fellow justices, ruled that Wade's victory was a constitutional precedent by a vote of 7–2. The justices were 8–1 in their decision to go out to dinner together after the fight, as long as Thurgood was picking up the check. Marshall dissented, but went along anyway.

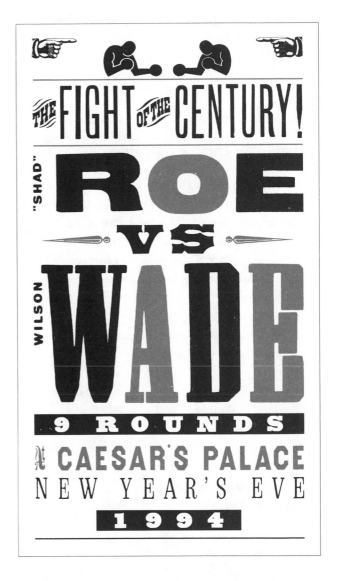

THE FIGHT OF THE CENTURY!

"SHAD" ROE

VS

WILSON WADE

9 ROUNDS

CAESAR'S PALACE

NEW YEAR'S EVE

1994

KIDS ON THE BLOCK

THE focus of the decade's most significant legal decisions has been on children and the reproductive rights of women ever since Levine v. Levine in '93 established the validity of a pregnant woman's claim seeking damages from her spouse for impregnating her. The following year, in a case that went all the way to the Supreme Court, Levine v. Levine established that embryos could be held liable for their actions in vivo.

The defendant in the previous suit became the plaintiff, charging the Levine embryo (which no longer existed, having become an eleven-month-old child) with alienation of affection. However, since O'Leary v. O'Leary of '92 had established that embryos are not entitled to own property, Mr. Levine (the father) was not awarded any damages.

Prenatal jurisprudence quickly became an integral part of law school curriculums, and those specializing in this newborn field soon became known as "pudenda defenders" or "pudes." Young and eager, these dispensers of intrauterine justice lost no time in bringing class actions against the manufacturers of birth

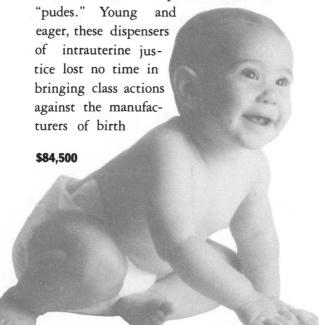

$84,500

control pills and any woman who suffered a miscarriage.

The discovery, in 1994, that the Heimlich maneuver induces abortion raised a clarion call from the pudes for an Embryo Bill of Rights. Heated controversy surrounded the question of whether it is possible, after the fact, to determine if a woman legally choked or illegally aborted. Predictably, liberal states like New York and California thought it wasn't, while conservative ones like Alabama and Utah took the opposite view. Of course, Las Vegas and Atlantic City are still the only places in the country where abortion remains legal and dentists the only professionals who perform them.

So many out-of-work dentists flocked to New Jersey and Nevada that price wars broke out, with one infamous doctor advertising a "Double Extraction Special: your unwanted tooth and fetus for only $29.95."

The most famous courtroom imbroglio of the 90s was, and continues to be, of course, the case of Baby O., whose New York father, an immensely wealthy illegal alien, willed his sperm shortly before his death in 1991 to a lesbian surrogate mother who lapsed into a terminal coma while undergoing artificial insemination.

Baby O. (now nine and a half) stands to inherit and make many millions of dollars when the details of his custody are settled. Nine parties have been battling for that right over the years—they include both paternal grandparents (who are divorced), each claiming ownership of the original sperm; the maternal grandparents (also divorced), each arguing for the egg; Mort Janklow, Baby O.'s literary agent; and the Catholic church, which holds that since the child was not conceived by sentient beings, he does not exist.

This tug of war over Baby O. was tame compared to that over Baby Pete. With infertility caused by artificial sweeteners affecting a third of all Americans, the practice of buying time-shares in babies grew enormously. Blond blue-eyed babies with one head were at such a premium that only those in the seven-figure range could afford their open market price. (Blond-blue-eyed-baby-with-one-head futures were the hottest item on the COMEX by 1996.)

Baby Pete, an unbearably cute BBEB w/OH from Dayton, Ohio, was typical of hot time-share babies. His time-shares had been sold on a daily basis in one-year blocks. While parents and baby agents routinely oversold their babies to some degree, expecting deaths, dropouts, no-shows, etc., Baby Pete's first 365 days on earth were owned by 7,314 people—all of them wealthy enough to afford his hefty $5,000-a-day tab.

The resulting lawsuit involved billions of dollars in emotional damages, murders-for-hire, and the additional complication that many owners of one-day time-shares in Baby Pete had "subdivided" their days into hours, and sold these tiny time-shares at enormous profits—all perfectly legally.

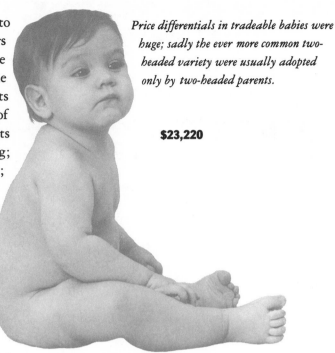

Price differentials in tradeable babies were huge; sadly the ever more common two-headed variety were usually adopted only by two-headed parents.

$23,220

Baby Pete is now seven, overweight, with mousy hair and crossed brown eyes, and is seriously disturbed. Thanks to the Kindergarten Bill of Rights and the Preteen Bill of Rights, his therapists are powerless to prevent what they reliably predict for his future: on his twelfth birthday, Baby Pete will murder them and his parents with a chainsaw.

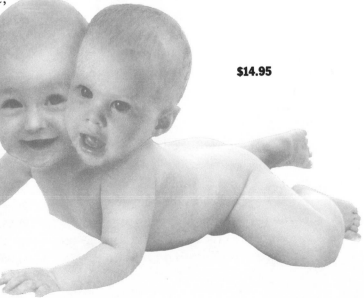

$14.95

THROW ONE FOR THE GIPPER

DOUGIE Drench stared out the window of his seventh-grade classroom. The May sun poured through the trees, the teacher droned on about characters and plot in the works of Tama Janowitz, but for Dougie, only the 1997 Lehigh League Baseball Championship mattered. The big game was today, and Dougie, the second baseman, had a job to do.

All week the two teams had rehearsed the game—just like in the big leagues. Two down, ninth inning, a sharply hit liner would roar straight at Dougie. He had to drop the ball—he just had to. If he forgot and made the catch, his baseball team would win, and that would mean that come the fall, the football team and the soccer team would lose the Lehigh League. No one would ever speak to him again. What a lot to ask of a twelve-year-old kid!

Sports in the nineties were like sports in the eighties—some sports. Picking up a cue from the certainty of professional wrestling and the commercial breaks of baseball, football, basketball, and everything else, athletic organizers found it easier for everyone to know in advance pretty much everything that was going to happen.

Consider this:

—Navy tight end Rock Greene knew his orders, and he was determined to carry them out. The call was for the bomb, and the defensive linebacker was a fool. Rock's task was to be sure the ball was intercepted—it wouldn't be easy, but it was crucial. No interception, no NBC commercial break right on time. No

commercial break, no pro career for Rock. The numbers were simple—the pressure intense.

—Olympic swimmer Valerie Splash stared with hatred at the East German girl. The papers had played up their rivalry for weeks—they screamed at each other at press conferences, spit at each other across restaurants. Angry partisan fans scuffled poolside and outside the doors. Now was the final heat, and if Valerie didn't punch the East German at the right moment in the final turn, the posters, the videos, the banners showing that slash—already printed and awaiting distribution—would be so much worthless junk. Her biography (which was already in the storage rooms of bookstores) would have to be scrapped and rewritten. Everything she and the East German had worked so hard to perfect would be ruined.

—"Stick" Simpson and "Stilt" Sorkin whispered over the book Stick had found. It was a 1988 National Basketball Association Rule book—and Stick and Stilt and eight other guys at North Dakota State used it when they snuck out onto the prairies to play "regulation" basketball. The Sigma Delts had caught ten

New and more realistic standards in baseball filtered down to the Little League:
here Mickey Roe of Cincinnati prepares to throw a game—and put himself through college.

other "turkeys" doing the same thing three years before. Those ten didn't play anything anymore . . .

And that's what they deserved—the cheating sneaks. Because if a bunch of guys can't behave in a sportsmanlike manner, then North Dakota State must be a pretty sorry place.

The glory of the Game–whatever it may be –was the focus of the 1990s. Human victory and human failure, excitement and action–sports distilled to its very essence. Whether under the lights at Wrigley Field or in a light snow in Green Bay, the dreams kids love to dream came true every day in the 1990s—dependably and on time.

TELEDUCATION

"**I LIKE** *the space shuttle because you can go to all the movies.*"

"*Spane is the capatull of Africa.*"

"*George Washington was president and he killed pirates with the magic whip.*"

These sentences were gleaned from the essay section of National Learning Attainment Examination (NLAE), which was given to all American high school students in 1990. The purpose of NLAE (pronounced "nuh-la-eh") was to determine once and for all just how stupid American kids had become. The answer: yikes!

In fact, teenagers had become so stupid that most of them no longer cared how stupid they were. Said a sophomore from Tenafly, New Jersey, "I think *you're* stupid."

The nation's parents and teachers were in despair until Secretary of Education Howard Hesseman addressed the issue upon his appointment in 1997. "The solution to our nation's educational problem has eluded us for thirty years," Hesseman said. "It's time for us to redefine the problem."

The only way to make the kids smarter, he said, would be to make the tests dumber. "Henceforth, Spane *will* be the capatull of Africa, and George Washington *will* fight pirates with a magic whip."

Traditionalists grumbled at first, but the overnight improvement in test scores made converts of all but the grumpiest skeptics. "All our students now score in the ninety-ninth percentile!" crowed one happy principal. "Most of them are so smart now that they don't even need to come to school. So they don't."

To reflect the nation's new commitment to excellence, textbooks were rewritten by the students themselves:

America lost the war in Vietnam because if you had an army full of bitter middle-aged beer-drinking men in wheelchairs you wouldn't expect to win would you?

The new textbooks looked nothing like the dreary tomes they replaced. Many were just a few pages long. Most contained blank sections for students to fill in themselves—if they wished to.

Predictably, pupil preferences center exclusively on television. But the educators have been quick to adapt. And redefine. Telehistory isn't history in any traditional sense, but it's better than no history at all. A pupil who snored through explanations of the Jurassic can grasp the concept of prehistory as expressed by the Flintstones. Literacy rates soar once literacy no longer involves *words*. Ditto SAT scores—when SAT stands for Screen Aptitude Test. Mr. Hesseman is now in his third season as guardian of the nation's young minds. A vastly popular figure, he is probably the first Secretary of Education in history known to America's pupils by his first name. Mr. Hesseman:

In the old days, people had a practical notion of a teacher as having had *experiences*. Of having actually done something giving him knowledge he would provide you with, should a similar event unfold in your life. But video has allowed us to feel that we've had so many more experiences than we've actually had, such knowledge on the part of a teacher is useless . . .

Of course you can put a book on film but what's so great about watching a lot of little words on a screen? I prefer to teach history with a remote control. You can focus on what's important. You can move from World War II to the American West to the present with a flick of the wrist . . .

Let's face it—you hear a lot about the Holocaust but it doesn't have the laughs that "Hogan's Heroes" does. On the other hand, telehistorians of World War II have never given Rick Jason or "Combat" their due. Bob Crane never had the guts Vic Morrow did . . .

My administration of this department will ensure that every pupil gets to see "Sesame Street" at least five times a day. He must be able to say his ABCs, count to ten, and tell one color from another, in order to be equipped for life in the shopping channels . . .

Teleducation is a force for world peace. Given the decrease in sub video skills, pupils no longer recognize shapes on a map, they can't read border notices and signs, they don't *know* where other places are. Naturally if you don't know where someplace is, you can't attack it. Telegeography is the greatest deterrent to war since nuclear weapons . . .

I don't think a pupil needs an attention span, and television is proof of that. It's a random conversational pattern. Sooner or later in my life I may have discussed just about everything and not said very much about anything . . . what was the question again?

I look at hieroglyphics as in one way a welcome throwback, in another as progressive thinking. We in teleducation call them pictolanguage. It's good because like television itself it gives the pupil a sense of movement—that something is happening when in fact nothing *is* happening . . .

If [pupils] want to learn about the practice of the law, that's a commitment of an hour each week for seven months with a review period through reruns. If they want to learn the history of the West, though, they're going to be involved with miniseries, and that means *prolonged* viewing . . .

It's true that it's good to be a little disturbed [in life], because then buying things can make you feel better. But there comes a point of diminishing returns. If you really start thinking about the human condition, chances are you're not going to go for that new Mixmaster...

I'm not going to say animals *need* television. I'm not going to say your average insect's life is going to be transformed simply because the industry finds a way to hook into a whole new consumer group. First of all animals don't have the money. But there were nay-sayers at the beginning of television who never saw the potential it held. Who's to say there couldn't be some fascinating programming directed specifically at the insect world or lower primates? Nature shows have always fascinated us. Why shouldn't there be some way to make them fascinating to the animals who've been the subject of them? That's the kind of aspiration I think teleducation can nurture...

I think kids who've gone to school under my administration demographically show more savvy about what's going on in the world of TV. They're more aware of shows that are working. More aware of the kind of audience samples that indicate why shows are working. And they have a better view of history, thanks in no small part to colorization, which brings the past more into the present...

If President [Rivera] said tomorrow, "Howard, you're leaving Teleducation. You're now Secretary of Defense," I could do a good job. I've played soldiers, I've played politicians. One of the advantages actors have is that while the average viewer believes he has had a wide variety of experiences through television, it's nothing compared to the wide variety of experiences the actor has simulated for the viewer.

=LOVE

=DOG (PITBULL)

=HAPPY (JAIL)

=FIGHT

KEITH HARING'S PICTIONARY

=MORE

=LESS

=TEACHER

=WEIRDO

=BOY

©1997
K. Haring

=GIRL

=NERD

THE WOODSTOCK BABY

SEPTEMBER 1992, I was working as a researcher on the Nestlés—Amnesty International Woodstock 25th Anniversary Show. A three-day global hookup with a full third of the profits, including merchandising, going to offset Nestlés' donation to third-world famine relief.

The "Woodstock baby" idea came out of an afternoon of "blue-skying." I wanted to do a series of profiles on all the Woodstock performers who had opened restaurants with cocaine money but that story had been told a dozen times.

"I came upon a child of god..." So when the baby angle came to light, I grabbed for it. There was so little known about this infant, the living embodiment of the Woodstock generation, that I knew it was the story that could make my career.

I found John Sebastian on the set of the *Welcome Back, Kotter* reunion movie. His announcement of the child's birth after Sha-Na-Na's performance was the only public record of the blessed event. Sebastian was little help. He had enough trouble remembering the lyrics to the theme he'd just written to this movie, let alone something back in the late 60s.

Fortunately, not all the Woodstock artists suffered from long-term memory loss. I met with "Country" Joe MacDonald at his wholesale furniture warehouse. He remembered the festival fondly. "One of the guys in our band

didn't listen to the PA and dropped a handful of brown acid. We had to talk him down for over an hour because the medical tent was all excited about this woman giving birth."

Luckily, Joe also remembered the doctor's name. It was the first clue in a nationwide search that ended in the last place I would have expected—Washington, D.C.

Sanford Ogden was a golden boy. Not yet twenty-five years old and already plucked from one of the most prestigious law firms in the nation's capital to head up a House investigative commission. He was young, handsome, wealthy, and obviously being groomed for great things. And then I walked into his office.

"We are stardust..."

All my evidence was circumstantial. Sanford claimed it was coincidence that he was put up for adoption at age one at the same orphanage to which I had tracked the Woodstock baby. He denied he had a dove-shaped birthmark on his shoulder. And he refused to allow us to perform a search for his biological parents. I can still remember him turning down the Muddy Atwaters CD to hiss at me, "I'm building a career here. I don't need some freeze-dried hippie turning my life upside-down."

"We are golden..."

The story ran as unsubstantiated rumor and the world ate it up. Right after that, the Democrats began running commercials intercutting snippets of one of his speeches with footage of Jimi Hendrix burning his guitar. His political career tumbled before the end of the year.

Sanford disappeared from the public eye in a cloud of embarrassment. He used his old connections and personal nest egg to amass one of the largest private fortunes in the world. When he emerged from his cocoon in 1998, he was ready to get back at the world that had borne and destroyed him . . .

Yasgur's farm smelled awful. Since he bought it, Sanford Ogden had allowed it to be used as a free dumping ground for every type of noxious waste known to man. I made my way up the winding path to Ogden's office on the spot where the bummer tent stood during the festival. His handyman, Alvin Lee, was defoliating the shrubbery by the door.

I had been seething with anger and guilt ever since Ogden's reemergence. But it was the letter that Ogden discovered and made public that made me decide to try and stop him. Like the story of his parentage, there was some doubt as to the authenticity of the letter but enough people believed it that it might as well have been true.

"And we've got to get ourselves back to the garden..."

I hadn't planned on using the gun. I just wanted to scare him. But Sanford wasn't scared. He greeted me with the superior politeness of a man with a mission. He was totally involved in what he had become. I was no

January 23, 1969

Dear Ahmet,

Jann Wenner assures me the concert is a go. We got the site and all the acts are signed. The way things are going, most of them won't live long enough to see how we package this thing. The film deal is a go and the dove logo is an easily recognizable icon perfect for merchandising. All the cards are in place.

Remember, your attitude should be benign disapproval at best. If the kids ever catch on that we're behind this, they'll drop it faster than the Bosstown sound.

All the best,

Micheal Lang

threat to him. He didn't blame me for what I had done. I merely "set him on the path of his holy task." He offered me a drink. When his maid, Melanie, came in, I went berserk.

Melanie "Lay Down Candles in the Rain, I've Got a Brand-New Pair of Roller Skates" Safka the voice of a generation, poet laureate to an age of dank college girls too lazy to read Sylvia Plath. And there she was, slipping ungracefully down the far slope of middle age in an overstuffed French maid's uniform. I unloaded four shells in Ogden's chest . . .

"We're not gonna take it; never did and never will..."

The arts and crafts room is warm and friendly. Santana's blue guitar seeps languidly from the corner speaker. I'm teaching some of my fellow patients the wonderful art of tie-dye. My days are peaceful. I have made a difference. I held a candle in the rain. I saved the Woodstock Age. I used a forty-five automatic to make sure peace and love shall never fade from the face of the earth.

POWER TO THE PEOPLE —the cry of the 90s—stretched the concept as never before. "Animals are people too!" claimed the NAAAP. "Why should prunes die to keep you regular?" thundered the vegetable rights activists. But it was women, through a canny non-confrontational movement known as femininism, who made the greatest strides. "Sure we want equality—we just don't want to be dikey about it" went a typical statement. Others followed—the homeless, the lifeless, all coming together in that great melting pot where there are no losers, and everyone's in charge.

POWER TO THE PEOPLE

Most dramatic moment in a dramatically femininist decade: the late Ayatollah's niece Deborah "Debbie" Khomeini became Ayatollah herself in 1992. She was known popularly as Big Imama.

Many hours were
wasted each
morning as
frustrated
chauffeurs
circled the
streets in search
of officials to
take to their
offices.

THE HOMELESS HAVE A PARTY!

THE surprise success story of the 90s was the emergence of homelessness as a growth industry.

Previously the homeless had been regarded as a national embarrassment. But now their prestige rose, and by 1996, people began referring to them by a new name reflecting their achievement—the majority.

Homelessness became chic. By mid-decade, most Americans tried to dress and act like homeless people even if they were not. The outstretched palm replaced the high-five as America's favorite greeting.

Admitting that one had a permanent dwelling became a faux pas and, fearing social ostracism, many homeowners knocked out their doors and windows and pretended to be squatters living illegally in abandoned dwellings.

Malcolm Forbes moved into a forty-six-room cardboard-and-tin shack designed by I.M. Pei and Maury Povich anchored the CBS All-Star Evening News from an abandoned 1968 Oldsmobile in the South Bronx.

Impeached by life: a rare shot of Ronald and Nancy Reagan in retirement.

Time Inc. launched an ambitious new magazine, *No Home and Garden*, aimed at 18 - to 34-year-old homeless people. It lost 58 million dollars because the subscribers had no address the magazine could be delivered to.

As homelessness became more popular, conscience-stricken yuppies instituted a Share the Pain program, vowing to spend one night a week on the street to show how much they cared.

This sudden influx of affluent young people occupied all available homeless shelters, train stations, junkyards, and sidewalk vents. As a result, real homeless people could find no place to sleep and many froze to death.

"I guess this will show that we're not as trendy and shallow as people say," one yuppie told *Outdoor Entertainment Tonight*.

One reason for these developments was the dramatic rise in the cost of housing. By 1992, it represented approximately 215 percent of the average family's income, a figure President Bush said was "perhaps a bit on the high side, though honestly it hasn't been a problem for me and Bar."

It was that year that the Homeless Party was founded. It achieved rapid success, electing many candidates to high office on the slogan "Got Any Spare Votes, Mister?"

Some of these homeless mayors and governors were highly effective in persuading Congress to allocate federal funds to the cities. But the Capitol corridors and steps became crowded with annoying, aggressive beggars, who could not be legally evicted as they were elected officials.

Others, however, had difficulty carrying out their duties. Many hours were wasted each morning as frustrated chauffeurs circled the streets in search of officials to take to their offices.

Still, some Americans secretly feared homelessness. For these, Prudential offered the nation's first homelessness insurance. Any policyholder losing his home was guaranteed a shopping cart, two shopping bags full of broken lamps, and a year's supply of Valium prescriptions and/or muscatel.

Following the government's lead Donald Trump hired hundreds of homeless people to work in his numerous residences as furniture. "They're surprisingly comfortable," Trump told *Unhoused People*. He added: "My beautiful and talented wife Ivana is personally in charge of feeding the furniture."

By 1998, however, the homeless suffered a sudden downturn in popularity as a newly emerging group, the lifeless, began to capture public attention.

Complaining of "unbelievably rotten conditions," lifeless people (also known as the breathing-impaired) began refusing to remain quietly in their graves as age-old tradition dictated. Their cause received a big boost when former president Ronald Reagan and his wife Nancy (both tragically crushed by a runaway robot shopping cart while picking through garbage outside a new automated supermarket in Playa del Rey, California, in 1995) assumed leadership of the movement.

"Death really didn't bother Ronnie," Mrs. Reagan confided to *Rigid People* magazine. "It wasn't a big change for him. As for me, sorry, but having to wear one dress for the rest of eternity was not something I was about to take lying down."

The historic first Stiff Lift televised concert held in 1999 at Los Angeles' Forest Lawn, featuring a jam session with John Lennon, Jimi Hendrix, Janis Joplin, Jim Morrison, Roy Orbison, and Mozart, raised a staggering nineteen billion dollars from concerned viewers around the world.

CHATEAU

"*Quiquebaque*" is what one Reagan-circle wit dubbed the Bel-Air mansion "friends" donated to the ex-president on his retirement in 1989. Reagan himself laughed out loud at the quip.

Despite growing reevaluation of his administration as little more than legalized looting of the public treasury, Reagan was convinced his Teflon was as tough as ever. He would repeat with glee his characterization by revisionist neo-con William Safire as a "lazy, sleazy, morally brain-dead blowhard, typical of the decline of *Homo americanus* in the late 20th century."

With homelessness reaching new highs, however, "Chateau Quiquebaque" began to sound a lot less amusing—especially to the Republicans. Just before the '92 elections, under intense pressure from his party, Reagan donated his mansion to the Bel-Air Green Acres Trust, and moved to more modest quarters in Santa Monica.

Hubris of another kind hastened Reagan's decline. His pet project was a remake of *Knute Rocke—All American* in which he would play not George Gipper but the legendary coach. He started to raise money for the movie, first signing with Vestron to do a daily wake-up show called "Brentwood A.M." (which was aborted after a week because Reagan wouldn't show up for work before noon), and then took a huge mortgage on his real-estate holdings.

The production was a fiasco. The Reagans' penury was compounded by the fact that neither of them had run a household budget for decades. Spurned by the children he spurned in the White House, shunned in the wake of the '92 election disasters by his "friends," Reagan declared bankruptcy in August 1993. Nancy spent the last of their funds trying to divorce him for "financial cruelty" and "gross senile imbecility." The judge turned her down. Sometime in the winter of '93, LA County Sheriffs evicted the Reagans from their Santa Monica home. After a brief stay in an SRO hotel in Venice they dropped out of sight.

RAISA, Benazir, Maggie, Cory, Marilyn, Imama Debbie—the She Decade's Honor List goes on and on. But none occupies so exalted a place as Pope Whoopi I.

The Church, bowing to global celebritization, decided upon the death of John Paul II, to elect its first showbiz Pontiff. The College of Cardinals' choice fell upon a layman, aging French actor Jean Paul Belmondo. Pope Jean Paul Belmondo reigned for a mere three months leaving the helm of the Church for a small role in the remake of Pierre Le Fou, in 1995. The Cardinals turned instead to another star, hoping with her election to entice disenchanted black and female Catholics back into the fold.

It worked miraculously. From the moment the Cardinals announced to the world "Habemus Papem" (using black smoke rather than white for the first time in history) the Whoop turned what she referred to as Holy Mothah Church on its ample rear-end.

She turned the Curia into a Vegas-style act (including the VatiCan-Can Dancers); she launched a worldwide confession hotline; she called for corporal punishment of all nuns by their pupils on the First Friday of each month. Her album "Rappin' with the Rock" went titanium (one billion copies sold) within weeks of its debut.

With the faithful streaming back to the Church by the millions, the Church had no option but to turn a blind eye to such innovations, but when Pope Whoop attempted to canonize the cast of "Star Trek," they decided things had gone too far. Despite massive protests across the world, she was defrocked and removed from the Apostolic See.

"The robe was too heavy anyway. I lost two inches in height," sniffed the ex-pontiff as she boarded a Concorde at Fiumicino to return to Hollywood. "But I wish Pope Whitney (Houston) the very best of luck."

THE ERRORISTS

WAY back in the 80s, a shrewd marketing expert noticed that similar people with similar purchasing habits tend to cluster together in the same areas.

Tobacco sharecroppers in Cud Ridge, Virginia, for instance, rarely send away for blown-glass figurines shaped like stylized puffins. And retired shipping magnates in East Hampton, New York, rarely ask their cooks to purchase canned refried beans that come with a spoon for quick, unheated eating.

In this perception lay the seeds of American demography. Only in the 90s did Americans finally begin to take pride in demography and in their particular demogroup. Brooks Brothers began monograming fourteen-digit democodes in lieu of initials for *White Collar Ex-Urbanites*. *Tornado Fodder*-types spelled out their democode numbers in plastic floral arrangements on the Astroturf lawns in front of their mobile homes. Professional sports teams split into smaller teams, each one representing one of their city's more powerful demogroups. The Boston Red Sox, for example, split into three teams: the *Tempermental Irish* Swingers, the *Irish-Hating Italian* Mick-Hitters and the *Tenure Track* Stat-Makers.

In many schools, children began to recite the Demographic Pledge of Allegiance. (They weren't required to by law, but the schools that did received better corporate sponsorship of their Little League teams and fresher milk in their cafeterias.) It went:

I pledge allegiance to the demogroup of which I am a living, breathing, purchasing member, and to the marketing/life-style concept for which it stands: one group of many, under constant scrutiny with frequent

adjustments according to new data, and equal purchasing opportunity for all (within the prescribed boundaries).

. . . And I was one man who would not take it anymore. I was in the *Squirming in Wealth* demographic code—made up of the sort of people who mock car phones but use them nonetheless, buy American unless Japanese is cheaper, watch Sunday morning news programs and are prone to ineffectual but self-satisfying displays of symbolic rebellion.

But that's not why I decided to undermine American demography. It's just that I wanted to meet some new people, people from different demogroups—a rebellious act in itself. We dedicated ourselves to spreading intentionally inaccurate and confusing data.

We called ourselves Errorists.

We ordered madras summer suits and wicker picnic baskets from the J. Crew catalog, and gave addresses in The Bronx and East LA. On the same order form, we sent away for complete silk tuxedoes *and* T-shirts with a drawing of a tuxedo front on them.

Every Friday, pretending to be a thousand different people from all across the nation, we phoned the disease center in Atlanta complaining of an icy feeling in the armpits and a painful itching sensation at the tips of our hair. As soon as armpit-warming salve and anesthetic shampoo hit the market, we dropped this, and instead began phoning in reports of scurvy outbreaks in Palm Beach, Florida, and smog hack in rural Montana.

And finally, we released our manifesto:

Errorist Manifesto

We are not the type of people who would usually do a thing like this.

We are not any type of people, in fact.

We are made up of people from all demogroups, united behind a common belief: that each individual human is different from every other human in every way. This we all believe.

We propose to give incorrect answers when contacted for random telephone interviews and to use an exasperated tone of voice while answering the questions. Not so exasperated a tone that the questioner will know that we're giving incorrect answers, but you get the idea.

We propose to return these United States to a time when people could buy what they wanted, and corporations had to make a concerted effort to attract, cajole, and persuade us—using commercials that featured attractive members of the opposite sex, an interesting cinematic style, subtly altered rock hits of yesteryear, plausible taste-test comparisons, and promotional giveaways of all sorts.

Some of us don't believe any of this, but most of us do. Sometimes.

When the next year's demography forecast charts came out, there was a new demogroup listed: *Errorists*. And soon after that came new breakfast cereals and computer bugs and nifty pants and other merchandise—all tailor-made to suit our *Erroristic* quirkiness. The demographers knew what we bought, what we watched, and how we felt. They knew that we were the type of people who hate to be lumped in with a group of other people exactly like us.

I and a few other ringleaders were rounded up by the Corporate Bureau of Investigation and quietly banished to hostile zip codes. Now I live in the Amish zip code from which I once "ordered" four hundred dozen pneumatic blush applicators. I have learned the error of my ways. As Winston Churchill is said to have once remarked to the Reverend Oprah Winfrey: "Demography may not be an ideal system, but it's the best one we have."

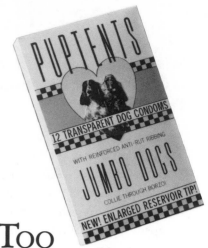

ANIMALS ARE PEOPLE TOO

SOME say that the lid really blew off in 1991—when self-proclaimed "animal language interpretors" claimed to read the lips of popular TV horse "Mr. Ed" and revealed him to be pleading, "Let my people go. *For God's sake, help me.*"

Others say that "Animal Rights" really got out of control when the U.S. Supreme Court voted to outlaw the wearing of dead animals "for any garment, or adornment purposes"—unless such decedents could be verified as "unintentionally squished or mashed by repeated vehicular traffic."

Who could really say when the rights of thinking, intelligent humans were completely eclipsed by those of four-legged creatures with the IQ of a smallish raisin?

"It happened because people became sick and tired of *other people*," recalls a former Animal Rights activist. *"Is that so terrible?"*

Evidently, it was. Who could guess in those innocent, heroic 80s years of saving bunnies from surgical scalpels that the Animal Rights movement would mushroom into something as vast and threatening as the "Animal Imperatives" movement.

Animal Rights became more than just a shrill, abrasive, self-righteous, dogmatic, fringe-style cause. It became a legitimate political party.

By the early 90s, the Animal Imperatives party was well-funded and savvy enough to run animal candidates for high public office.

The 90s saw the first arctic hare to declare candidacy for state senate. The first female Lhasa apso to sit in the House of Representatives. The first hawk on the National Security Council. (He ate the dove). The first weasel to *not* embezzle money from the New York City Board of Estimate.

Success and power led to vicious party infighting. Blood and fur samples were drawn on more than one occasion. "We got bogged down in semantics," recalls one party organizer. "We couldn't say 'dogmatic' without correcting it to 'dog and/or cat-matic.' We got into stupid tangent discussions about 'invertebrate rights.'"

PITBULLS ON CRACK

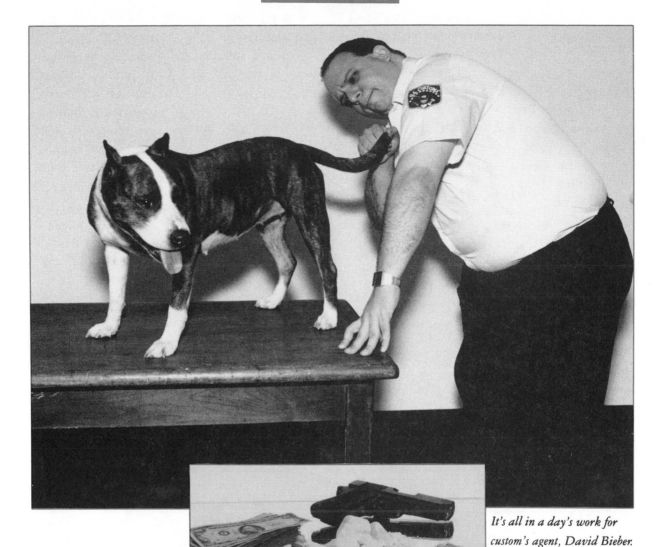

It's all in a day's work for custom's agent, David Bieber. The pitbull, George, was convicted of smuggling three pounds of cocaine, assorted handguns and $100,000 in cash.

Epithets such as "bull-shit," "hogwash," and "dog-face" became grounds for discriminatory suits. Everyone began to think and feel with increased "animo-consciousness."

A number of pets became highly sensitized to patronizing (or "pet-ist") language, and this became a highly visible issue.

Animals let it be known that they preferred the term "animo-Americans" to "pets"—an issue which in printing costs alone began to hobble the American economy.

The word "endangered" replaced the word "bad" as a hip term denoting coolness in music or dress. (As in "That's an *endangered* guitar solo, dude.")

The animal R & B charts were dominated for years by Blind Pogo McFarland, "the Blues-Harp Seal"—he of the scorching solo rendition, "I Be Endangered."

The term "endangered species" was increasingly seen as simplistic. A series of gradations developed, beginning with "endangered species," down through "overworked species," "underexposed species," and "socially inhibited species" to "somewhat annoyed species" and "fed-up species." Zoos were rendered obsolete in '92 — and became "animo - day - care centers," with giant waiting lists for spoiled, acquisitive "YUPPETS" (Young, Upwardly Mobile Pets).

As for people (when they dared show their faces at all), they affected the practice of wearing drugged, *live* animals to social events. This wreaked havoc in coat - check rooms, when hopelessly stoned bags, stoles, and accessories were found having wild sex in unprecedented combinations.

The drugs wore off, too, with often devastating results: it became known as the "Cinderella effect."

"One minute I'm schmoozing with Mike Ovitz, the next minute the bearskin rug is regaining consciousness and eating Bernie Brillstein," recalled one prominent show-biz animal attorney. "My homeowner's premium tripled."

"I think it's out of line," said Wolfgang Puck of the fast-gourmet chain McSpago. "I'm seeing animals coming into my places wearing people. I mean, what kind of statement are they making? I think it makes them look fat."

It became foolish in the nineties, on a social level, to ever contradict the truism "Animals can *so* talk and read and write, just like the goddamn rest of us."

"Animal interpreters" became a huge segment of the educated U.S. public. Animal celebrities had huge phalanxes of "human interpreters"as well as the ubiquitous "handlers," "feeders," and "walkers."

"It's a matter of trust," one of the animal interpreters vouchsafed. "Yes, we *could* be making it all up. But then, you'll never know, will you? Ha ha ha ha."

Eventually, popular entertainers like Lassie, Rin-Tin - Tin, and Flipper were widely shunned as "animal stereotypes." "The old Amos and Andy syndrome," said one attorney for the NAAAP (National Association for the Advancement of Animo-People).

Animals were given the right to attend medical school. To pilot airplanes. To work as fashion models and air-conditioning and refrigeration experts. To become firefighters. To bear the children of humans. In one famous case, a surrogate mother bore the dog-boy of another couple, who were unable to have a puppy themselves (due to the husband's allergies).

The Katma Sutra was a wildly popular small-mammal sex-manual demonstrating scores of positions for Master's lingam and Kitty's yoni.

THEY BEHAVED LIKE ANIMALS

IT is an historical fact that the formation of any rights group is first and foremost sexually motivated. Civil rights meant people wanted interracial sex; gay rights meant they wanted gay sex. It was no different with animal rights.

Having sex with animals, however, involved some unprecedented complications. On the one hand, for perhaps the first time in history men with miniscule penises were objects of envy. On the other, the specter of pet-AIDS stalked the hydrants and hot tin roofs of America. The widespread use of dog- and cat-condoms helped, but as street-pet populations grew so did the health problems. (Ironically, many animals ended up on the streets because people not wishing to demean their pets by keeping them as pets let them go). It was inevitable too that some of these street-creatures found their way to drug use. Although IV-ing drugs was still beyond the motor skills of most pets, the introduction of various consumer lines such as pet-wine, pet-cigarettes, and pet-snuff during the early nineties gave them the expertise to experiment widely with controlled substances, leading in turn to uncontrolled rutting and the further spread of disease. It also caused the social problem of human-rape by animals. Drug-crazed ex-pets (in one case a puma) were frequently arrested for molesting humans, particularly under-age humans. (Eventually a cure for pet-AIDS was discovered, after extensive experiments using homeless people as subjects.)

TOURRORISM

ON a macroeconomic level, the most important development of the 1990s was the rise of the consumer retribution movement. Within this spectrum, no single group occupies a more important place than the retributive tourist, or "tourrorist."

Tourism attained its current status as a vehicle for social retribution because of widespread disgust with the state of international air travel in the early 1990s. By 1992, terrorism had reached a fever pitch. Airline regulations required that baggage be checked two weeks in advance and that passengers be chained in their seats. Those in first class were escorted to the lavatory by armed guards; those in economy class were forced to use potties and beakers ($4 if bought separately; $1.50 if purchased with headset).

Capitalizing on public revulsion at such indignities, Mohammar Khaddaffi launched a hugely successful travel network of terrorist-free flights to Europe and the Middle East. Yasir Arafat followed suit with his equally successful West Bank-based airline "El Pal." Curbside baggage check was once again possible and travelers could visit the toilet in peace. Service expanded to cover the globe and major carriers such as TWA, Pan Am and Air France were forced out of the international market.

At this point, the true face of Islamic tourism manifested itself. Air Khaddaffi tore all the seats out of its fleet of 747s and replaced them with prayer mats, requiring travelers to kneel, facing Mecca, for the entire eight-hour flight to Europe. Moreover, all international flights, even quasi-domestic ones (e.g. Los Angeles–Mexico City), were forced to lay over at the world's largest hub, Medina. On El Pal in 1992, male tourists were even subjected to in-flight circumcisions ($4 separately; $1.50 with headset).

On December 4, 1993, tourists finally struck back. Declaring, "We'd rather die on our feet than sight-see on our knees," a group of irate Kiwanis Club members overpowered the security "stewardesses" on a DC-10 bound for Tahiti hurling them to a watery death in the Eastern Mediterranean. The effect was electrifying. Emboldened tourists everywhere flexed their muscles. Khaddaffi and Arafat were quickly forced out of the travel market, and when hijackers reappeared, they were routinely stomped into insensibility by mobs of militant tourists.

"The age of the pussy tourist is over," declared Bobby-Thor Johnson, publisher of Now Voyager, a newsletter for retributive tourists. "It's payback time."

"Parlez-vous, my ass." Georgina McGovern, *a leader in the Tourrorism Movement, exacts revenge for decades of insolent service.*

For many months, the friskiness of the tourist community generated positive results. The skies truly became friendly. But then tourists began exploiting their hitherto hidden strength and sought revenge for decades of linguistic humiliation, misdirection and overcharging. In August 1994, more than half a million Midwestern executives and their families descended on New York City and rode the subways for several days, making it impossible for native New Yorkers to get to work, go home, shop or even mug one another.

"We were sick of the $18.95 hamburgers and signs saying 'Restrooms Are for Patrons Only,'" said Eunice Gladden, retired silo salesperson. "So we figured, let's inconvenience these bastards for a while."

News of the epic prank spread. Soon other aggrieved wanderers, alerted via newsletters (AirHustler, Tourist of Fortune, Frequent Josher) and electronic bulletin boards, jumped on the bandwagon. In Italy, an estimated one million Japanese tourists took turns rocking the Tower of Pisa until it collapsed. Meanwhile, hundreds of thousands of polyester-clad tourists surrounded the Tanglewood Music Festival in the Berkshires, repeatedly chanting, "Hey, Did You Happen to See the Most Beautiful Girl in the World?" while the Boston Symphony Orchestra unsuccessfully tried to perform "The Rite of Spring."

Winter 1994 brought a brief respite. But it

was only to organize the supreme act of tourist retribution. On Easter Day, 1995, spurred by cheap "April-in-Paris" fares to Europe, over twenty million tourists from all over the world arrived in France and spent the weekend trashing the entire country.

In every hotel along the Cote d'Azur, bidets were ripped from bathrooms and tossed into the street. Food-fights were staged in every restaurant with two stars or more from the Michelin Guide Bleu. Vintage wines were sent back with cigarette butts stuffed in the neck. In Paris, thousands swarmed onto the *bateaux mouches* until they sank. The Eiffel Tower disappeared under a mountain of toilet paper. Accordions, berets and bikes were burned in huge bonfires in every Place de Ville. Those who objected were "cheese and feathered"–smeared with overripe Camembert and rolled in used Kleenex.

Said Jean-Claude Danquin, author of *Tourist with a Human Face* (himself a victim of a brutal saucisson stabbing), "Basically every man, woman and child in France was tourrorized during 'The Normandy Invasion.' The general feeling seemed to be that the French had had this coming for a long time."

Cinq ans après, militant tourists still see their original mission as untarnished. "The Khaddaffis of the world are always with us," said one retired pharmacist from Phoenix recently. "The price of freedom is eternal vigilantism."

THE BIG ONE makes people happy and nervous. Sure, it's 5760 if you're Jewish. And of course Asians call this year "2000" simply as a courtesy to lost European hegemony. But the prospect of history's odometer rolling around by three zeroes has sent an earthquake of expectation across the planet.

THE BIG ONE

Divine media manifestations
are becoming more common as the Millennium approaches,
often accompanied by elaborate special effects on-screen and off.

FINAL DAYS—EVERYTHING MUST GO

FROM a religious point of view, the last decade of the second millennium A.D. was as frenzied and bizarre as the final years of the first. Apocalyptic movements swept across America, strange prophets arose, strange portents were seen. To many, the powers and principalities seemed to be walking the earth in expectation of the Day of Judgment. And for every honest seeker trying to find out if there was any truth in all of this, was another who was trying to find out if there was any money in it.

September 22, 1991, saw the discovery, at a swap meet in suburban Memphis, of the miraculous Shroud of Elvis. The lavish, sequin-encrusted cape is said to be the last garment worn by the Saint, and bears an imprint of his sorrowful face. Tania Wicks, who got the shroud in exchange for an almost new microwave ("the beeper was busted") had been looking for a Dracula costume for her son, Terry.

"When I got home and saw his blessed face and sideburns, I trembled all over and fell to my knees and prayed . . ."

The seriously overweight Tania's faith was rewarded. By week's end, she had dropped forty pounds. (Son Terry lost twenty-two.) Miracles swept her neighborhood. Most involved dramatic weight loss, but some included the removal of facial hair, warts, large moles, even harelips. Doctors were unable to explain the phenomena. Experts from Xerox and Kodak couldn't identify the process by which the Saint's likeness had been transferred to the fabric of the Shroud.

Elvis' sanctity was firmly established and

the Presleyterian Church has flourished ever since. Presleyterians take as particularly significant the Gospel text in which Christ promised: "Upon this Rock I will build my church." In imitation of the Cathedral of the Shroud (formerly Graceland) many churches boast an authentic relic of Elvis, some of them undoubtedly spurious. At one point five separate churches claimed to have the Saint's Pelvis.

Less successful though just as numerous has been a millennial group called the Flatulents. Originating in retirement communities along Florida's Gulf Coast, the Flatulents move from town to town in large groups, humiliating themselves by breaking wind in public. Many communities, citing air-quality standards, have passed ordinances against the Flatulents, but the movement has enjoyed great popularity amongst senior citizens, to whom it offers an easy, and frequent, method of performing penance. The Trumps of Doom, as they call themselves, have become a common sight in the South, as have the mass prayer meetings at which thousands chorus the "Our Farter." The

*A million miracles and counting. The Shroud of Elvis has been identified
by carbon-dating experts as the actual cape worn by the Saint when he ascended into heaven from the Blessed Toilet.*

movement is believed to have its origin in a misunderstanding of the word *flagellant*.

In sharp contrast is a movement known as "bored-again Christianity." Bored-again Christians cite many causes for their disaffection: televangelist scandals, the proliferation of messiahs, Japanese acquisition of major Christian sects. Jimmy Carter, who, according to some telehistorians, was once president of the United States, now owns a chain of successful bored-again pool halls. He blames ruthless exploitation of the Apocalypse. "A man has only one Second Coming in his heart," he says, "and once that's used up, he feels like smoking a cigarette. There's nothing to live for but pool and whiskey. Praise the Void."

MEDIAPOCALYPSE

IF—as a few determined souls still believe—the Messiah appears tomorrow, He or She will find that as far as the media is concerned, the end of the world is last week's news.

At the other end of the decade, things were different. As former ABC news chief Roone Arledge (now serving ten-to-twenty for aggravated reenactment at Fort Boesky) said in 1991: "The Apocalypse is a once-in-a-lifetime news op. Plus it's great entertainment. Many-headed beasts, scarlet women, the cries of the damned. Good guys, bad guys, fabulous effects."

Arledge's campaign to "lock up" the Apocalypse ran into a brick wall, however, over the essentially theological question of who owned the rights to it. Rome and Constantinople, on the point of reconciliation after a thousand years of schism, reopened the wounds of the first millennium in a bitter copyright battle over whose "employee-for-hire" St. John had been when he wrote the Book of Revelation. (The Patriarch pointed out with some justice that Patmos was unquestionably in his territory.)

The situation was complicated when CBS News czar Howard Stringer (now serving fifteen-to-life on seven counts of telecide at Milkenworth) started a bidding war. And further so by an angry denunciation from the British-American fundamentalist consortium of Revs. Jerry Falwell and Iain Paisley. Since the Pope of Rome was the Antichrist, Paisley said, "he'll do everything in his power to get the cameras pointing the wrong way on The Day." Falwell-Paisley PLC offered the networks a package including not just the exact time and place of the Judgment, but a name-the-names list of the damned. This in turn was challenged by the Jehovah's Witnesses, who claimed Judgment was only a week away, and by the Mormons who claimed it would happen in Utah and produced a contract with the Lord written on a dinner plate. Confusion was complete.

Eventually everyone cut a deal. But the subsequent exploitation led quickly to saturation. Sneak previews, countdown shows, tabloid programming (e.g., Fox's "It's a Revelation" and "Lifestyles of the Rich and Damned") strained the public's tolerance. The Vatican's belated entry into the field with its Plenary Indulgence Shopping Channel and World Confession Hotline did nothing to help. One HD-TV manufacturer claimed his product gave so superior a picture of reality that it defined the essence of things and therefore of God.

God, in fact, may well feel that in this welter of apocalyptic programming, the real thing is not being given enough exposure. But video faith is unlike the old-fashioned kind. With video faith, the more you see, the less you believe. Thus the great beast reported in May 1998 to be slouching toward Bethlehem, PA, was written off as a corporate publicity stunt. The "Christ" executed earlier this year

It walks, it talks, it damns you to all eternity. Popular amongst fundamentalist parents, the Beast of Revelations Toy brings the Apocalypse home to toddlers.

in Israel was dismissed as a charlatan simply *because* his apparent resurrection was recorded on videotape. Ditto with the following account of a recent divine media manifestation, which occurred last Christmas in the United Kingdom. It is reported by the celebrated raconteur Graham, Lord Chapman of Chapman:

On December 25, 1999, God, wearing a lime-green anorak and air-cushion sneakers, manifested Himself in a two-hour heavenly inspired telethon, dubbed by the press as the Godathon or the Thon of Thons.

He won startled viewers over easily to His initial claim that "This is God speaking" by the use of blood-red skies and the fact that His voice made people's bones vibrate. The Holy entity had a captive audience, the ratings dipping only after the first six minutes of each segment in accordance with the limits of human attention spans.

Most critical reaction to the show was predictably sycophantic. However, fundamentalists were angered at God's temerity in claiming fallibility. They were outraged when He admitted that "things haven't quite worked out as I'd hoped in the last 2000 years, but as a forgiving God"—and this is what really stuck in their craw—"I hope people will now try harder to think well of each other."

There were some doubters, of course. Scientists could not accept the divinity of the broadcast on the basis of one isolated appearance, even with admittedly remarkable special effects. Atheists wondered if a real God would have used earthquakes to underline a statement about our duty to enhance the ecosphere, but many of them were won over by His apology for mocking their beliefs.

He went altogether too far for the meek, though, when He hinted that the universe might as well end tomorrow if all life forms fail to realize that they are in this thing together. They thought it most unGodlike to emphasize this statement in such a loud voice that it may have been quite frightening to those of a nervous disposition, although of course, it might not.

RESULTS OF THE WORLDWIDE MAN OF THE MILLENNIUM CONTEST

LIBYA
Mummar Khadafy
Moammar Kadhafy
Mummar Kadafi
Calvin Klein
Mummar Khaddaffi
Mummar Kaddafy
Mummar Khadafi
Galileo
Mummar Quaddaffi
Mummar Quadafi

KOREA
Kim Il Soong
Sun Myung Moon
Johnny Yuen
Tran Van Ko
Calvin Klein
Kim Bong Ho
Jeff Altman
Yu Ohk Lee
Galileo
Richard Allen

UGANDA
Idi Amin
Milton Obote
Whitney Houston
Nelson Mandela
Kwame Nkrumah
Patrice Lumumba
Kareem Abdul–Jabaar
Galileo
Tarzan
Eddie Murphy

FRANCE
Napoleon
Joan of Arc
Charles de Gaulle
Jerry Lewis
Louis XIV/
 Victor Hugo (tie)
Brigitte Bardot
Calvin Klein
Monet/Manet (tie)

IRELAND
Sean O'Faolin
Sean O'Grady
Sean Young
Sean Connery
Sean Lennon
Calvin Klein
Sweet Rosie O'Grady
Galileo
The Edge
The Bog

NORWAY
Galileo
Roald Amundson
Edvard Grieg
Dag Hammarskjold
Hendrik Ibsen
Knute Rockne
Jerry Lee Lewis
Calvin Klein
Thor Heyerdahl
Bob Denver

JAPAN
Thomas Edison
Marconi
Henry Ford
Vincent Van Gogh
Galileo
Michael Jackson
Steve Lawrence &
 Edie (1 vote)
Walt Disney
Calvin Klein
Hirohito

NICARAGUA
Bianca Jagger
Barbara Carrera
Fawn Hall
Sylvester Stallone/
 Oliver North (tie)
George Bush
Bud McFarland
The Sultan of Brunei

Galileo
Calvin Klein

AUSTRALIA
Yvonne Goolagong
John Newcombe
Rod Laver
Fred Stoller
Arthur Ashe
Ivan Lendl
Billie Jean King
Bud Collins
Galileo
Calvin Klein

AUSTRALIA
Roseanne Barr
Robert Blake
Andrew Dice Clay
Morton Downey Jr.
Fosters lager (big cans)
Galileo
Jacko the EverReady
 Guy
Calvin Klein
Geraldo Rivera
Al Sharpton

YUGOSLAVIA
Josef Broz Tito
Mrs. Jovanka Tito
Zdravko Tito
Miroslav L. Tito
Vesjelko ("Bobo") Tito
Mt. T./ Mr. Ito.
Calvin Klein
Tito Jackson
Galileo

ENGLAND
Liverpool United (FA
 Cups Winners
 1989/1999 season)
The Page 3 Girl
Calvin Klein
Elvis

King Chuck the Equal
Wilfred Pickles
Galileo
John Merrick, the
 elephant man

ITALY
Pope Whoopi the Ist.
Galileo
Benito Mussolini
Fabian
Marconi
Mario Puzo
Marco Polo
Gina Lollabrigida
Botticelli
Marlon Brando

CHINA
Mark Rudd
Ling Ling
Emanuel Lewis
General Tsao
General Tsao's Chicken
Warner Oland
Calvin Klein
Mao Tse Tung
Walt Whitman

ISRAEL
Madonna* (as Blonde)
May Britt
Anita Ekberg
Britt Ekland
Ursula Andress
Bo Derek
John Derek
Calvin Klein
Copernicus
Galileo

USA
Calvin Klein
His Honor, Bill Murray
Spuds Mackenzie
Jack Ruby

Elvis
Susan Lucci
Col. Sanders
The cast of the
 Fantasticks
Galileo
MacRuff, the Crime Dog

CANADA
William Shatner
Bobby Hull
Bobby Orr
John Diefenbaker
Galileo
Robert Goulet
Boom Boom Geoffrion
Margaret Thatcher
Sara Lee
Wayne & Shuster

RUSSIA
Peter the Great
Calvin Klein
Yaakov Smirnoff
Copernicus
Billy Joel
Olga Korbut
Leo Tolstoy
Omar Sharif
Julie Christie
Levi Strauss

BRAZIL
Antonio Carlos Jobim
Pele
Jorge Ben
Calvin Klein
Caetano Veloso's
 and Bethania's mother
Gal Costa
Christopher Columbus/
 Gilberto Gil (tie)
Dorival Caymmi
Thomas Edison
Joao Gilberto/
 Stan Getz/Galileo (tie)

THE WINNERS—GALILEO AND CALVIN KLEIN

I PREDICTED THE FUTURE

by Penn Jillette

THE information on the next couple of pages is not very startling today. A quick check-in to any data base you were allowed to access would yield these same names and numbers. But what if I told you the information on the next two pages was written over 10 years ago?

I'm a psychic. In early 1989, I was still ambulatory and free to go wherever I wanted in Manhattan. Tony Hendra called and told me that he was editing a "look back" of the 1990s and he wanted me to be his first contributor. I was to use my psychic powers to "look back in advance." His idea was for me to write my chapter of the book in 1989 and have it sealed until the rest of the book was done in the year 2000. He wanted nothing but hard facts. "Major assassination in the middle of the decade" wouldn't cut it. He wanted names, dates, times....he wanted Superbowl scores.

I wrote over 1,000 predictions in a flurry of psi. In December of 1989 I delivered the predictions to Tony in a sealed envelope. The predictions were locked in a vault. Five years later, when banks went out of business, the predictions were moved to a prison. Three years later, when jails were moved underwater, the predictions ended up in a locked desk at the publisher's. In January of this year, 2000, I took them home to tally the results.

I was happy with my predictions. I picked the ones for publication that were the most impressive. Some of the others were true but hard to test ("There will be a top secret project that will produce invisible insects that live without eating"). Some were too personal to be of global interest ("Penn Jillette will be sleeping with the cute check-out clerk at the 7-11 by late 1992").

The statistical evaluations were done by Chip Denman of the University of Maryland.

LOTTO
First Jackpot over 100 Million—1990
The winner will be a 23-year-old German man who works at a One Hour Photo developing.

Dead on. Early 20s, foreign, service industry.

Super Bowl XXV—January 1991
Washington Redskins–27
Chicago Bears–10

I call this a "hit" even though one of the teams is wrong because the chances of hitting the first time is 1 out of 29 and the point spread WAS within 9. As a sad side note it was the '97 Super Bowl that I had the best feeling about and I lost my shirt on Cincinnati.

Hurricane "Fabian" Late August 1991
will rock Florida

Dead hit. "Rock" may have been a little exaggerated but the name and time were right on.

June 25, 1994
Cure for common cold announced by
Upjohn Pharmaceutical

So we all still have runny noses, but a U.S. company did announce a new anti-viral medicine. That's a hit.

Kentucky Derby—May 6, 1995
Winner's purse $781,700

Dead hit. I said the purse would be the highest ever.

Academy Awards 1997—No prediction made.

In 1997 the Academy Awards were cancelled. I call this a hit because I predicted nothing. And that's what happened.

Boy, is my face red!
Biggest Blunder of the 1,000

Imagine when I looked at the little slip of paper that said, "The Pope will be shot dead on March 5th, 1995." Wow, sometimes we hit—sometimes we miss. I'm still hiding my head on this one.

In early 1998, a small group of dedicated computer scientists, pooled their talents to generate a millennium song that would underscore the cultural contributions of various ethnic groups in the United States.

The project dubbed ART (America's Rich Tapestry) solicited direct input from the countries of origin. Then–with an eye towards thematic and commercial unity–they fed the result or "epthnic poem" into a CompHost 2100 Sequential Quantizor. This, as the group put it, "streamlined the great Rainbow of lyrical diversity, into one bright white Light of American unity."

The song was a massive hit throughout the United States (and possessions). In the rest of the world, the recording inexplicably stiffed.

It is presented here in its "Before" or Rainbow version; and in its "After" or SQUART version.

SQUART–THE SONG VERSION 1

Now the glowing embers drop from
Time's smouldering rope in a smelly heap. *(Romania)*
A great wind-barking unicorn, surnamed Freedom,
Froths like the mad Adriatic. *(Yugoslavia)*
Look! Oh, see! There rises a nation
Great and warm and toxic! *(Pakistan)*

The rolling hills, where tomatoes burst open
With natural and artificial coloring, plenty for all! *(Italy)*

At this Millennial juncture let us celebrate
The truly alarming goodness of such a place. *(Denmark)*
We pull many boner in past times,
Now we are all friends and can fish together. *(Vietnam)*
The Seed of Demos, the Egg of Athena,
Render that Zygote which is Zeus' unto Zeus, okay, Sport? *(Greece)*
We come as moths to your diverse Metropoles: New York, Chicago, New Orleans, and don't forget the Motor City. *(Zaire)*

To pull up stakes and furl our tents in the night
And flee the fearsome moderate elements of government. *(Iran)*
To yank out anchoring pegs and collapse our shelters in the dark
And flee the fearsome moderate elements of government. *(Iraq)*
To challenge the bull, to dice for Don Q.'s damp mufti.
To take a quick lunch in the shade of Liberty's cork tree. *(Spain)*
To raise our voices, and hear voices raised in answer!
To be a Man! To smash the state just a little bit! *(Poland)*

CHORUS:
We came for the food. We came for the food.
We came for the food. And the kids like the rides.
(Afghanistan, Argentina, Brazil, Cambodia, Ethiopia, Hungary, India, Mexico, Puerto Rico, Sri Lanka, Syria, Thailand, Turkey, Uganda, Uruguay, Yemen)

This is America's Century. Not the Fatherland's as we once hoped;
But as the kinder say these days, "sheiss happens!" *(Germany)*
And though the world has seemingly forgot
I-AM-bic PENT-a-ME-ter, WE have NOT! *(Great Britain)*
A little café, devoid of bourgeois comforts and processed foods,
Is squeezed to death by Wall Street. What pity! *(France)*
We're fine. Don't worry about us. We don't need a thing.
A phone call would be nice, if it's not too much trouble. *(Israel)*

REPEAT CHORUS
(Bolivia, Canada, Chile, El Salvador, Philippines)
The rhythm of the children in a rub-a-dub style,
The monkey chewed tobacco at the Mercantile. *(Jamaica)*
The stinking corpses of free men block the Gates of Paradise,
And you're not even paying bloody attention! *(Ireland)*
But here in the Cradle of the Dollar, this Laissez-faerieland!
The Sun always rises, except for a few scary moments. *(Switzerland)*
And speaking of The Rising Sun, we take pride in our New Status
As Custodians of The Future for The United States! *(Japan)*

REPEAT CHORUS
(Australia, China, Cuba, Czechoslovakia, Dominican Republic, Egypt, Guatemala, Haiti, Lebanon, Libya, Panama, Soviet Union, Sweden, Taiwan, Zimbabwe

SQUART–THE SONG VERSION 2

Don't really care
If you're black or white or brown;
Or if beige or ochre's your nat'ral hue.
It's a MACRO kind of love, Syntactic'ly aligned;
An interface 'twixt user port and you!

CHORUS
You are the world!
We are The Country!
We are the host and you're the guest,
Just bank that mem'ry.
You're a billion points of light,
But we supply the juice!
We're the cube, the root,
The Great Hypoteneuse!

Repeat Chorus ad infinitum, or to taste.

THE MOP SONG 2000

BY DONALD FAGEN

Say Mop-d'dwee-dit
The sky is falling
Men of Earth
Your time is up
We have come
To decorate your world
To mopify your planet
Say Moppity-mop-d'dwee-dit

Say celebration
Der Himmel fällt
Hombres de la Tierra
Votre temps est fini
It's party time
But first a thorough cleaning
We'll mopify your planet
Say Moppity-mop-d'dwee-dit

Our leader told us
That y'all are psycho
That soon you'll be
Right in our face
Say Hallelujah
The Fire-Mop is hungry
We'll mopify your planet
Say Moppity-mop-d'dwee-dit

Music and Lyrics by:
Stend'or of the Rill
c/o S.S. Revelation
102nd Starfleet
Sector 1267H4
Earth Orbit 10021

MILLENNIUM

BY HERB SARGENT

Millennium-Yum-Yum
Millennium-Yum-Yum
Millennium-Yum-Yum
Millennium-Yum-Yum

Hey
Unfurrow your brows and

Welcome two thousand
Say no to millennium blues

We're gonna be heroes
By two and three zeroes
We've paid our millennium dues

Just cause the century's
Ready for denture
re-pairs
There's no use for abuse of
A Deuce and three goose
eggs
Who cares?

So
Take a few bows and
Beat swords into ploughs and
Welcome two thousand with
cheer

Spread the word through the
land
That the brand new two grand
The two-triple-oh is near!

Should old acquaintance be
forgot
The two-oh-oh-oh is here!!

PINK DISH RAG

BY RANDY NEWMAN

When I hold you in my arms
I think about the night we met
I never wanted that night to
end
But it did, but it did.

BRIDGE:
Why did you treat me so bad?
Why did you use me as if I
were
A foolish little pink dish rag
You could throw about with
impunity?
(Won't you) Dance with me (one
more time)

(Won't you) Dance with me.

(Repeat Chorus)

Pink Dish Rag from the
No. 1 + album "Terri" April
1999, Warner Bros. Records.

"When I was a kid I was very
influenced by 10,000 Maniacs.
I loved their music and the way
that even though it didn't
always rhyme, it all fit
together and made sense. But,
I also loved to dance and I
couldn't do that very well to
their music though I had a
friend who could."

Interview–Terri–Rolling Stone
May 1998.

DUKE OF EARTH

BY DAVID FRISCHBERG

We're number one!
We're number one!
Of all the solar system
We're the baddest planet in it!
Ain't no planet out there
Start a war and hope to win it!
Ten billion fingers jabbin'
Up to the sun!
Check us out, mother-fuckers!
'Cause we're number one!
We're number one!
We're number one!
We're number one!
We're number one!
We're number one!
We're number one!
We're number one!
We're number one!
We're number one!

(Repeat and fade with track)

THE MILLENNIUM SONG

BY JONATHAN WEIDMAN

(Intro)

The clock strikes midnight,
Somber bong
We raise a glass,
Ten billion strong
One thousand A.D.
Hey, hey, hey,
It seems like only
yesterday . . .

(Verse)

Millennium, millennium
We sing in praise of
thee-oh!
We raise our wine to Calvin
Klein
Salut! stout Galile-o!

If past is prologue, holy
cow!
The last grand never bored
us.
The Borgias, Hitler, Donald
Duck,
The future lies before us.

(Chorus)

Oh, thousand years of
hopes and fears!
Oh, thousand years! oh, joy!
Oh, thousand years of japes
and jeers!
Oh, thousand years!
oh, boy!

T R U M P

THE SHOT HEARD 'ROUND THE WORLD

DONALD Trump, by the time of his 50th birthday, had become the world's most notorious recluse. He lived alone with his third wife, Cornelia Guest Trump in the Trump Triplex atop Trump Tower and it was said that they hadn't had a visitor in more than three years. Word had it that Trump's wispy, shoulder-length blond hair had grayed and become brittle; that his fingernails, which he refused to cut, had become gnarled and hideously twisted. It was said that he stored his urine in 10-liter mason jars which he then stowed away in vast underground vaults beneath Trump Tower.

IN HIS feral, delusionary madness the trillionaire seized upon the idea of upstaging the end-of-the-millennium celebrations in Cairo, by dismantling one of the pyramids, shipping it across the ocean and reassembling it in Central Park. An army of engineers and more than twenty thousand men were flown to Egypt to dismantle the great pyramid stone by stone. One hundred oil tankers brought it to New York

Harbor. For months, 42nd Street was unusable as legions of flatbed trucks ferried the pyramid to the park.

WOULD anyone who attended the celebrations ever forget them—especially their horrifying conclusion? There, against the backdrop of the towers along Central Park West, and covering most of the Great Lawn, loomed the haunting figure of the pyramid. Every Scots pipe band that could be hired was flown across the Atlantic. The food, which was laid out on 100-yard banquet tables, was sufficient, it was estimated, to feed the Sudan for a dozen years.

IF EVER there was a center of the earth and of all eternity, this surely was it. When the crowd began a ten-minute countdown to the millennium's end, armed members of the Trump Guard turned 10,000-kilowatt searchlights on the heavens. (Soviet cosmonauts stationed on the Moon claimed later to have seen the glow.) At the stroke of one minute to midnight, there was a deafening hush as Trump, through massive loudspeakers he had installed in the Triplex—and relayed around the world via Trump Satellite hookup—ordered the whole city to endure a minute of silence. Then, one second before midnight, the jittery cool night air was ripped by the amplified sound of a single gunshot. As the report sped 'round the planet, every head in the park turned to where the shot came from—the Triplex atop Trump Tower! The century, the millennium and the Age of Trump, were over.

**Looking
Forward**

Picture a classroom in the year 2090. A class is preparing for its final examination on its "sister" period, just one hundred years before.

The astute teacher turns to an anxious youth, "Yes, Doug," she says, "what is it . . . ?"

"There are two things I still don't understand," he says, "about the 1990s."

"And what might they be?" she says.

"the resale of Alaska to the Soviet Union . . . "

"Yes . . . "

"And the statute granting protected status to 'Women's Writing.' "

"Let me deal with both your queries at once, if I may," she says "what would you do, if you had a vast, unusable mass of oil-soaked material . . ?"

"Yes," he says, "but what about Alaska . . . ?"

**with
David
Mamet**

HAVE A NICE MILLENNIUM!